Social 2010

Teens Tell It Like It Is Series:

I Wish I Knew What To Do?!

On What To Say To Get Bullies To Leave You Alone!

Edited by

Beth Carls and Amy Looper
with Jennifer O'Brien

The MindOH! Foundation
www.mindohfoundation.org

Published by The MindOH! Foundation, Houston, TX
Printed by DiscPro Printing and Graphics, Houston, TX

Copyright © 2005 by The MindOH! Foundation
ISBN 0-9773689-0-4

$14.95 USA $22.95 Canada

Publisher: MindOH! Foundation
            2525 Robinhood
            Houston, TX 77005-2511
            www.mindohfoundation.org

Creative Direction: Amy Looper
Project Management: Jonti Bolles
Inside Book Design: Jonti Bolles and Jennifer Vodvarka
Cover Design and Illustrations: Darci Mostaert

Dedication

*We dedicate this book to all people from 7 to 70 who
have felt helpless and hopeless in the face of bullying.
And to our families for their love and support.*

Table of Contents

3. CHARACTER LESSONS

4. CYBERBULLYING

5. THE GOLDEN RULE

8. TAKE ACTION

9. TEACHABLE MOMENTS

10. THE BULLY

Acknowledgements

Since 2002, The MindOH! Foundation and MindOH! have been privileged to work with dedicated students, educators, non-profit organizations and socially responsible corporations to create The Character's Cool Contest (CCC). Over the past 4 years we have touched thousands of students' lives and they have touched us back with their honesty and ideas on how to improve their world. Without the dedication of the following people, the first book in the *Teens Tell It Like It Is* series would not have been possible.

The person with the initial idea for the Character's Cool Contest and the one who has nurtured it over its entire existence is Jennifer O'Brien. Jen deserves a huge amount of credit for helping create the venue which would make this book possible. Thank you, Jennifer. We're honored by your dedication and commitment to help kids, MindOH! and the MindOH! Foundation.

Our deepest appreciation to our fellow co-founder, Leslie Matula. Leslie has worked tirelessly over the past 15 years to advocate for youth. In doing so, she unwittingly has become a national subject matter expert in the field of character education. She has supported, contributed and nurtured our collective vision to help students, educators and parents in many areas, inside and outside the Foundation and the company, in addition to this book. Her devotion and insights have been a keystone with the MindOH! team.

We would like to send a special "thank you" to our 2005 essay contestants and survey participants and especially to the 95 special teen authors whose stories can be found in this issue: Lorna Abner, Courtney Andries, Morgan Elisabeth Ayers, Emily Bees, Jeremy B. Buhain, Tyson Bybee, Amanda Carey, Jeffrey Carter, Zi Wen Chen, Katelin Chow, Carmen Adriana Clemente, Kathryn A. Costidis, Amanda Daly, Tram Dao, Jennifer Dragobratovich, Natalie Dumsha, Heather Dyer, Robert Emfield, Megan Faherty, Devin T. Fields, Brittany M. Folsom, Megan E. Fox, Katelyn Frost, Carlee Gabrisch, Shae Goldston, Holly Golia, Maria Grekowicz, Kerrie Haurin, Emily Hazzard, Ann John, Christopher Johnson, Jamie Leigh Jutrzonka, Miranda Kafantaris, Swara Kantaria, Vicki Kasza, Will Kearney, Stacey M. Keller, Delphine Kirk, Kylee Knights, Katelyn Koble, Jon Lakoduk, Nicole Le Boeuf, Audrey Lindsey, Janet Little, Erika Loesch, Katie Magness, Kristina Maiello, Garrett Maner, Grace McConville, Nicole McDermott, Laura McFee, Rachelle Melancon, Kelsey Mullins, Juan Munoz, Liza Navarro, Rachael Olan, Michael Olan, Jackie Pajor, Youngmin Park, Cassandra Pastorelle, Elyse Pizzo, Mary Ann Presutti, Jessica Prior, Beverly Reed, Tiffany Renert, Taylor Rexrode, Logan Riley, Marissa Robinson, Kayla J. Rohaley, Stephanie Rolz, Lisa Scougall, Kate Sheehan, Alyssa Tia Sherer, Jonathan Sinkkanen, Brooklyn Dawn Smith, Anthony James Smith, Alyssa Solak, Samantha Soto, Matthew Spicer, Taylor Michelle Syslo,

Holly Tamburro, Tyson Taylor, Meg Taylor, Zachary Jordan Teter, Kristofer J. Thompson, Hanh Truong, Taylor Nicole Turner, Laura Urbanovich, Matthew Webber, Kelly Wilde, Michael Willen, Susanna Winder, Joey Zigarelli.

All those who read the original essays and served as judges for our 2005 Character's Cool Contest: Amy Looper, Ammy Sriyunyongwat, Angela Graham, Beth Carls, Briana Barcelo, Brooks Tutor, Drew Carls, Ed Kirk, Elizabeth Van Auken, Erin Brady, Herman Chan, Jean Smith-Wooley, Jennifer O'Brien, Jennifer Vodvarka, Karen Zent, Kathy Guenther, Keith Rudy, Kim Hart, Kimberly Tutor, Kris Hines, Leslie Matula, Lydia Wacasey, Mari Hirabayashi, Marsha McAnear, Michelle Garrison, Pat O'Brien, Phuong Phan, Phyllis Berger, Suzanne Johnson, Val Turner and Weston Carls. There were a lot of essays, and you pulled through in spite of an already full schedule of your own! Thank you!

To our 2005 Character's Cool Contest sponsors and financial donors – Athletes for a Better World, Bobbie and Richard Kristinik, Freddie and Marsha McAnear, Gil and Norma Luton, Joe Vodvarka, John Coleman, Mind Over Machines, MindOH!, Mothers Against Violence in America (MAVIA), Project Wisdom, Ric and Kathy Guenther, Ron Monford, Students Against Violence Everywhere (SAVE), Suzanne Johnsen, Terrell and Audrey Hitchison on behalf of Richard Luton, and The Center for Safe and Responsible Internet Use – for without your financial and in-kind support this contest would have not been possible.

To the MindOH! team – Brooks Tutor, Jennifer Vodvarka, Jonti Bolles, Judy Levin, Kathy Guenther, Kris Hines – who handled things at the office so we were able to make this book happen. The MindOH! Board of Managers has been tremendously helpful and supportive over the years. Thank you for all the meetings you've attended, the budgets you've reviewed, the support you've given and the connections you've made for us – Alicia Goodrow, Charles DeLacey, Dr. Kelly Trlica, and Ken Olan.

Additional thanks go to the following friends:

Dr. Beth Manke, Dr. Ernestine Riggs, Janet Pozmantier, Dr. Jean Smith-Wooley, Dr. Joyce Gayles, Dr. Linne Bourget, Dr. Marvin Berkowitz, Cheryl Gholar, Elizabeth Van Auken, Karen Zent, Dr. Michelle Rabin, and Dr. Sandy Bushburg for their expert opinions and contributions on our Content Review Sub-Committee.

Terry Simmons at Thompson+Knight, for his brilliant legal mind in the field of charitable organization giving and his continued support of the MindOH! Foundation.

Allen Fahden for your friendship and whose creative brilliance is super-human. The Character's Cool Contest "Bully?" "No Bully?" campaign creative was a home run. To Karen Zent for your friendship and invaluable feedback and numerous contributions, as well as, being our keeper of all things politically correct! To Ken Olan, "Mr. Flashpoint", for your friendship, brilliant creative and collaborative genius. To Sam Horn for your wisdom and guidance to help produce this book. To Jerry Bass, our longtime friend who got this book printed and delivered in less than 10 working days during Hurricane Rita!

To our friends and alliances in the mission to help kids succeed. We value your individual missions and collective energies: Michele Pola, Nan Varoga and Jon Forde, The Houston A+ Challenge; Sara Selber, The Philanthropic Management Team; Rosanna Moreno, Wells Fargo Bank; Janet Pozmantier and team at ChildBuilders; Michael and Lisa Holthouse, The Holthouse Foundation for Kids and After-School All Stars; Brian Cruver and Brett Andrews,

Giveline; and Pat Rosenberg, The Search Institute.

Because this is our first book project and it was a huge undertaking, we are sure we have left out the names of some of the people who helped us. We apologize and are grateful to each and every one of you who have supported our collective mission to help our nation's kids become successful and thriving citizens.

Preface

If you've picked up this book, one of several things might be going on for you. You're getting it for a teenager in your life that you love and care about who has either been bullied, been a bully or is telling you some frightening things about what they've seen happen to other kids.

Regardless of the reason, it's a good thing you are doing for them. By buying them this book, it will let them know that you want to start the dialogue with them on these topics. You're now initiating the opportunity to fix the problem *with* them, not for them.

The statistics are staggering. What we've uncovered from our 2005 Character's Cool Contest Survey will surprise you. Especially the information about a new, more emotionally harmful form of bullying – *cyberbullying*. We've found that kids are just not telling adults about cyberbullying or most of the other bullying that affects them daily. In fact, 82% of the kids in our Survey said they'd either been bullied, have bullied or witnessed bullying.

Why are kids not talking about this? Simply, regarding cyberbullying, in some cases they don't want their computer privileges taken away. Regarding the more traditional bullying issues, they don't think the adults around them will understand or can do much about it.

What we found from the voices in these essays is that kids want the adults in their lives who care about them to help them. They just don't know *how to ask you* for the help without worrying about what you'll do about it – like taking their computer privileges away. They've told us they want to work together with adults to create a solution. "Give us the tools ... ," wrote one middle school writer.

The essays included in *I Wish I Knew What To Do* give insightful advice and suggestions from the kids themselves on how to help them work through these issues – whether they are the bully, the bystander or the victim.

> *"If you love yourself enough and believe that you're perfect the way you are, others will recognize that and not bully you. You can't expect others to love you, if you can't love yourself first."*
>
> *By Kate Sheehan, age 15, CT*

Through the publication of these teens' bullying experiences, our goal is to have adults become more aware of the pressing bullying problem. We support anyone reading this book to seek out resources to deal with this issue.

Once you've had time to read these students' essays and review the recommended resources, we'd appreciate knowing what you think. Please let us know of good resources you might have found – we'd love to review them for inclusion in the next printing of the book. You can reach us at beth.carls@mindoh.com or amy.looper@mindoh.com.

Beth Carls
Amy Looper
Houston, Texas, September 2005

Introduction

Why did we do this book? Because we care about what kids think and we believe they actually hold a lot of the answers to the questions adults keep trying to figure out for them. They've told us that adults frequently don't listen to them and that makes it harder for them to talk to us.

Through our work at The MindOH! Foundation, we've consistently seen that if we take the time to ask kids what's on their minds we'll get remarkably candid feedback. If we simply value and validate the kids in our lives by bringing them into the conversation, listening to what they know and actively working to come up with a solution together, they will readily and willingly participate.

Additionally, we have observed over the past four years that we all need to listen to our teens about things that concern them – we're now starting the dialogue with a bullying book written for teens and by teens.

Thousands of teens from across the country have participated in the Character's Cool Essay Contest and Survey since 2002 and shared their feelings about current events affecting them. Many of these issues are things we adults had no clue about how hurtful and long-lasting the impact can be to our teens.

In a feedback survey of teachers and administrators that participated in the 2005 Contest, 79% said that bullying was a problem on their campus, 86% said the theme sparked school wide or classroom discussions about bullying, and 100% said they would recommend the Character's Cool Contest to other educators.

The Foundation has received tremendous support from school districts, departments of education and other educational organizations across the country. Year after year, these organizations continue to come back to promote and participate in the MindOH! Foundation's Character's Cool Contest and Survey. For more information about the 2006 Survey and Contest please see additional information at the back of the book.

The Department of Education recently said that "bullying can interfere with learning and often leads to greater and prolonged violence. Research and experience suggests that comprehensive action involving teachers and other school staff, students, parents, and community members are likely to be more effective than purely classroom-based approaches."

Until 2005, many of us didn't know the alarming statistics around cyberbullying. How many of you adults had ever heard of the word cyberbullying before today? Cyberbullying is harassing, humiliating, intimidating and/or threatening others on the Internet. Some teens are using the Internet to deliver cruel and harmful messages. Sometimes cyberbullying involves racial, religious or cultural slurs. Sometimes it is sexual in nature. It can involve someone you know or a complete stranger. The stories in this book are written for teens and by teens to raise awareness about bullying and its consequences.

One writer who recently interviewed us for an article commented, "I didn't know what cyberbullying was. I decided to ask my 11-year-old son if he knew about it. To my shock and surprise, he said 'Yes.' And I thought I monitored his computer usage well."

It's our hope that these teens' words and wisdom will get the dialogue started on both sides in order for them to feel comfortable talking about the effects bullying and cyberbullying are having on them. Most importantly, we hope that adults will pay attention, value them and make changes happen to provide safer environments – at home, in the classroom and on the playground.

Amy Looper
Beth Carls
Jennifer O'Brien

How to Use This Book

While it may seem silly for us to make this suggestion, anthology books, by nature, allow you to simply pick up the book and start reading any story you flip to, reading what ever speaks to you at that moment in time. Actually, that's a really great way to use this book. We've found over the years that when we have something on our minds we're trying to figure out, we can simply read about how that particular topic was handled by someone else.

It's like having a mentor right at your finger tips. Most of us think mentoring involves only face-to-face interactions with a person – usually an adult. We believe you can also receive the benefits of mentoring through a book like this. Editing this book has allowed us to learn so much from kids involved in bullying every day.

For kids, this book is a great way to get some ideas or suggestions for help to share with a trusted adult mentor to start conversations.

For adults, it needs to be a wake up call – we need to pay more attention to what teens want us to know about bullying – even when they can't quite say it to us directly.

So, kids here's how we think you could use this book:

Flip through it, get a feel for the chapter topics. These are topics written for you by your peers to learn from, to get inspired from and, in some cases, it just may be the nudge you need to take action against bullying.

At the beginning of each chapter, we've provided an exercise for you to ponder. It's offered as a way to get you thinking and moving forward on something you can do for yourself or someone close to you. We hope you'll write your answers and thoughts down so that this becomes a reference for you when you need it most. Don't worry about spelling or being neat or writing what you think someone else wants you to say. Write what you think you need. Just write!

Read the stories over again that speak to you. Each time you re-read a story something will become clearer or you'll pick up another nugget of information that might be the missing piece you need to solve what's on your mind. Underline or highlight what speaks to you. Write your thoughts out in the margins. This is your book. Use it!

If the messages are making sense to you, you might want to make some changes in your life. In fact, a lot of our teen authors offer advice about what they've learned through their personal experiences. It's always easier to make small changes here and there rather than making them all at once.

After you've read a story you may want to lay the book aside and give yourself some time to think. Run your thoughts by an adult you trust. Go back and write down what you want to commit to change to help the bullying situation you may be faced with – either as a victim, a by-stander or maybe to help you stop bullying someone else.

Experience tells us that if you take a few specific things you want to change, write them down and then record the results as you go, plus take 100% responsibility for your actions, you'll begin to see positive changes that will become a habit for you.

So parents and other adults, here's how we think you could use this book:

Use this book to start the conversation with those teens in your life who need resources, help and acknowledgement of how to deal with this serious and growing issue.

As parents ourselves, we've taken books just like this, read the stories and written comments on what we wanted our kids to know when they read the same stories. Some anecdotal, some in question form – "Have you had this ever happen to you? This happened to me once." Or maybe, "Have any of your friends ever had this happen to them?" Sometimes that's all that's needed to get a conversation started.

Dr. Phil advises in his book, "Family First," "making sure your children see that they are being heard is extremely important in ensuring you too will be heard. Bottom line: You have to listen to be heard."

Good advice.

Amy Looper
Beth Carls

Chapter: 1 Accepting Diversity

In the space below, list a few ideas to increase diversity awareness among you and your friends.

What Every Big Sister Wants

I have witnessed many bullying incidents. Even though they now have a rule in our school about bullying that results in serious consequences, nobody really reports it. Sometimes I see people bullying and I want to put a stop to it, but I don't have the guts. When it comes to my friends and family though, I definitely step in.

My younger sister Melissa is in sixth grade. She has learning disabilities and learns slower than the average person. She is her own person and acts like she doesn't care too much about what other people think about her. Melissa is also a little smaller than most kids her age. To bullies, Melissa is an easy target.

I babysit her friend Sarah once and a while, and Sarah tells me things about the bullies. They leave my sister out at recess so she plays by herself. People in the group that she is friends with say that the others can't play with her. People talk about her and put her down, make fun of her. Most of the time they don't do it to her face, just behind her back. When people do bully her to her face, she gets upset.

Sometimes she comes home upset and I have to get it out of her. She tells me that somebody pushed her today, or called her a name. My parents went to her teachers and the teachers have put a stop to the bullying they see, but they can't be everywhere. Lately not really anyone has bullied her that I know of, which is good. Kids are mean, so they probably start rumors and talk behind her back to make people think she's weird.

Whenever I see someone bullying her, I go up to her and I say, "Hey Melissa, who's this?" When they see me they usually stop talking because I'm bigger than them. Or if someone is talking about her and I hear it, I ask them to stop. It gets me really mad when they bully her because I want what every big sister wants for their little sister. I want her to be happy and fit in without having to worry about other people putting her down. Unfortunately, that's not the reality. Melissa will probably be picked on her whole life because she's different. She doesn't mean to be or want to be, but she is. I try to help as much as I can, but she also has to learn to fend for herself. In high school she will be a freshman when I'm a senior so I'll be able to look after her more, but I can't always be there for her.

I hope people will realize she just wants to fit in and she's not doing anything to them, so they will just leave her alone. I hope when they're bullied, they will realize what they are doing to her. I hope people realize that my sister is just like them, unique and trying to fit in.

by Amanda Carey, 14
Glastonbury High School
Glastonbury, CT

Bullying: Calling it Quits

Bullying is a horrible habit that must be broken before the bullied turn to violent revenge for help. I think that the worst types of bullying are racial, weight, and intelligence related bullying. I believe this because of what can result from physical and psychological damage that both the bully and his/her victims sustain from violent acts and verbal threats in these situations. In general, bullying is wrong for anyone's self-esteem.

Racial bullying is one of the most common reasons that people are bullied today. People should stop judging other people on their skin color. At this time, race determines how you're supposedly living. For example, if you're of African-American ethnicity, you are said to have grown up in a broken home and are eventually going to become a part of a gang or something much similar. If you are Caucasian, you are said to grow up in a normal home where you grow up to be rich, or at least upper middle class. But there are people who don't like that they are stereotyped and decide to change, most likely resulting in that person becoming a bully to those who are then below them.

Bullying someone based on the fact that they are obese is

also wrong, and could cause both people (bully/victim)to feel damaged. This could easily result in physical and psychological damage because of what the obese person may think when they hear that people don't like their weight. It could cause the victims to become anorexic or bulimic and hurt themselves just to appear thinner. Of course, in the end, the victim will have destroyed their digestive system and broken away some of their esophagus, and most of their self-esteem, having resorted to self-abuse. The bully, after the victim has nearly killed himself to please everyone else, may feel responsible for anything that happens to the victim in the future, and may never be able to live with him/herself.

Intelligence is another reason that people are bullied. This is, also, another type of bullying that goes both ways. If the bully happens to be smart, then his/her victim is going to be on the side of lesser intelligence. But if the bully isn't very smart, then his/her victim is going to be on the intelligent side. This may do nothing to the victim's grades, but it does have a large amount of pressure on the victim's self-esteem.

To be more general, appearance has a large part in bullying. Eye-problems, braces, clothing style, personal style, and vocal inability, are common points. Bullies try to find pleasure by taking their anger out on people that are mentally and emotionally stable, hoping to make these individual people feel less and less about themselves so the bullies can feel more masculine around their victims.

Bullying is a problem that needs to be taken care of before things get too deep. For example, most school-shootings are related to the fact that the shooters have been bullied or torn down and decide to ultimately overpower their bullies. This, of course, is not the way to solve problems. Usually in the said situation, more than just the bullies get hurt.

We need to call bullying quits. Of course, I say "we" in a larger scale. We, children and adults, should, together, put an end to bullying by helping the bully rather than punish him. Forcing him/her to stop is a waste of time. With force, the bully will ignore everything that they are told. But if you try to address the problem in a more finessed way, they will slowly ease into the fact that they have to learn a more positive way to deal with their anger. Those are all of my reasons for wanting to put an ultimate end to bullying and my take on how we should try to help bullies call it quits. Bullying is not something that the world needs right now. There are way more important things to be worrying about. It has to stop.

By Nicole Le Boeuf, 13
Franklin Middle School
Nutley, NJ

The Back of the Bus

Bullying in schools among peers has always been a problem. From kindergarten through high school, the older or more popular kids are always pushing around others. One particular bullying incident stands out in my mind. I witnessed it on my school bus.

Everything seems to happen in the back of the bus; away from supervision. There were five boys the same age as me who sat in the back of the bus. Three of these boys were of Middle Eastern descent. Although at first, the boys seemed to get along fine, as the year progressed, they began to pick on each other more and more. One of the boys in particular, the one with the most Middle Eastern appearance, seemed to be pushed around the most. The other guys would call him names and take his things. They often grabbed his hat or backpack and would throw it around the bus. He tried to laugh with them because they used to be his friends, but it was getting harder everyday. Every afternoon on the bus, the harassment would pick up right where it left off the day before. I didn't understand why two boys also of the same race would make fun of another boy with the same ethnicity for being that race. They were in fact putting down their own heritage. The only reason I can come up with would be that they too were embarrassed to be different and didn't want to be made fun of.

The name calling turned violent in several occasions, although no one was ever seriously physically hurt. The other four would start by pushing the one boy or by taking his hat. They would throw his possessions around the bus and would refuse to give them back. They would then shove him in his seat or pin him down. There was not much he could do besides just trying to push them off. He was probably the same size if not bigger than each of the bullies, but they outnumbered him 4 to 1. They kicked him in his seat and slapped his head. I know I should've stood up more for the kid and I wish I had.

On several occasions however I did get his hat or bag back from the others and told them how immature they were acting. I wasn't scared of them because I knew the kids and knew that they were pretty harmless. They didn't retaliate that I had given the kid back his things, they just appeared annoyed that I had ruined their entertainment for the day. The bullying and harassment eventually died down, but not until after friendships had long since been broken and the victim was completely demoralized.

As far as preventing another similar event from happening again, I don't think there is that much that adults can do. They are constantly giving lectures and talks in school about bullying, but it doesn't really ever seem to sink in. Bullying between peers has been going on forever. There's no way the busdriver could've known what was going on.

One thing that could possibly be done to help prevent bullying on buses in the future would be to have a second adult on the bus at all times. Therefore they could pay attention to what was going on with the kids. I know this is already done to monitor some buses, but it is not on every bus. It needs to be, because the back of the bus is a popular place for bullying to occur.

By Heather Dyer, 14
Glastonbury High School
Glastonbury, CT

Infect the World with Peace

As a seventh grader in a new school, I was afraid that I would not fit in. Suddenly, my worst fear became a reality. On the first day of school, I took the school bus with my aunt and my mom. When I stepped onto the bus, I was met with the words, "Look at that Chinese kid. She can't even take the bus by herself." I was deeply embarrassed. We sat down on the front seats and ignored the kids on the bus. But they continued to taunt me and bully me, all throughout the bus ride.

This is an account of a time when I was being bullied. I did not even know the kids on the bus, but yet I was bullied anyway. To understand my situation, we must step back and examine the nature of bullying. Wikipedia defines bullying as "a form of harassment associated with being performed by a child who is older, stronger, or otherwise more powerful socially, upon weaker peers." Bullying is the immoral act of harassing another person. It is bad and it is wrong. It comes in many different forms, from calling people names to beating on other people. Bullies may be big, small, short, or tall.

But they all have a purpose in mind: to cause pain for the

bullied person. They may think that they are tough and superior to the person who is being bullied. They may think that they are popular and fit in with their group of "tough guys." They may think that they are releasing their own pains by causing pain upon other people. But all of these thoughts are wrong. To cause happiness for themselves, they must stop bullying and make other people happy. As Lord Byron once said, "All who would win joy must share it." That was the first day of school and I was already feeling sad and unwelcome.

At school, however, I did find plenty of friends. I became happier. To evade the situation I was in, I had decided to break away from the bullies.

As Benjamin Disraeli, the famous British novelist and prime minister, said, "There is no happiness without action." But what I did not do was to tell a responsible adult about this. If I had told a responsible adult, the kids would learn to stop bullying. If the two kids at Columbine High School had told someone about how they were being bullied, they would not have resorted to violence. If we spread the words about tolerance and respect for others, bullying will become history. A famous Chinese proverb tells us that "the person who removes a mountain begins by carrying away small stones." Peace is contagious. We must first take the step to infect others with peace and instill respect and tolerance. Bullying can be stopped.

By Zi Wen Chen, 17
Boston Latin School
Boston, MA

Do, Re, Me

Bullies bully people who feel insecure about themselves. That's why it's the disabled, the mentally challenged, and the bookworms who are the targets. I was picked on because I had bug-eyed glasses and strange clothes. I was larger and overly eccentric to top it all off, and I'm Korean, which accounted for racism. As long as I turned red and hung my head, the bullies kept picking at me like vultures. Being the "strange" kid wasn't easy, and the teasing continued from elementary to middle school.

There were a bunch of boys in town who went on my bus every day. They were typical teenage boys; interested in sports, pretty girls, and very egotistical. In fact, when others thought they were complimenting me, they were really just getting their kicks from my helplessness. Swan was my nickname. It was coined by a bully I had in fourth grade, and it was revived again during middle school.

Six boys ambled onto the bus, making obscene jokes and punching each other. I was in the back of the bus. Yesterday, I had received a solo for my upcoming choral concert, and announced it on the bus ... a big mistake.

"Swan, why don't you sing for us?" one boy turned to face me, his eyes smirking. I froze. I was proud of my singing; what was this guy trying to get at? Another boy spun around. "C'mon, Swanster, give us a few notes! I think you should be on American Idol!" My first instinct was to beam. Almost immediately, I doubted myself. I couldn't be THAT good, solo or not. The bus was silent. It was the morning; I was bound to croak. It'd be better to stay silent. I shook my head, slouching in my seat.

Disappointment filled the air. The whining started. A girl in front of me turned around. "Kate, sing. They won't stop." Everyone else nodded. What else could I do? The whole bus was against me, and ten minutes were left of the bus ride. As I opened my mouth, my throat went tight. The silence was suffocating, and I wanted to cry.

I sang softly, my voice quivering. My hands clenched as the boys leaned over to each other, snickering. I knew it, they were just ridiculing me! As the notes got higher, I sang more meekly, starting to mumble. Finally, my voice cracked and they burst into laughter. It was the most horrible experience. I buried my face in my hands. I always failed, what good was I? I was bound to a life of humiliation.

Later in the school year, I started to change. I began to like myself. My solo in the concert went well but I wanted to be even better, so I signed up for voice lessons at a professional studio.

Eventually, I changed items in my life I had control over. I got smaller glasses that made me look pretty, not nerdy, and I started watching what I ate and became thinner. My body was changing by itself as well, and looked more graceful, not awkward.

My self-confidence transcended, and the boys on my bus saw the change. Soon, I decided to show them who was boss. I sang once more at the end of the school year, and this time, I didn't croak. One boy and I even ended up becoming friends in the following year. I noticed the difference, and I wondered why and how I had changed so much. I didn't change myself on the inside; I wasn't at all friends with the popular girls in my school. I didn't wear makeup ... some of my clothes were bought from Salvation Army. What was different?

Then came the realization. Bullies pick on kids who don't love themselves; that had been my problem all along. When I started finding my true self, I began to see what the real me liked, and I reveled in it. I found someone who I was comfortable being, and I liked myself.

The boys on my bus still call me Swan, and I think it's a cool nickname. I know I can't change some things, so I accept them with grace because I know bullies don't target someone who's confident. If you love yourself enough and believe that you're perfect the way you are, others will recognize that and not bully you.

You can't expect others to love you, if you can't love yourself first.

By Kate Sheehan, 15
Glastonbury High School
Glastonbury, CT

How One Incident Led to Many

This is a story about a young girl who was born and raised in Newark. When she was nine, she went to a school on 13th Ave. She was nice to everyone. She never bothered anyone.

One day, this boy came up to her and pushed her face into the mud. When she got up she asked him what did she do to deserve that. He looked her straight in the eye and told her that he did not like her because she was a teacher's pet and because of the way she looked.

The next day, the same boy had everyone messing with her and calling her a teacher's pet. They would push her, pinch her, touch her, take her things, throw things at her, take her pens and other things that belonged to her and throw them back at her. They would even take her glasses and throw them in the trash. Every week something bad would happen to her.

When she turned eleven, she thought things would be better. She came to find out that things got worse. People would tell her she had no taste in clothes and no taste in anything. They even told her that she would never get anywhere in life because she was dumb. They would also call her a "white cracker." Some boys she knew, would follow her home and throw things at her and spit on her.

One night in October, the boys had everyone come to her house and throw frozen eggs, frozen batteries, and even rocks. Some boys got caught and were charged with assault but others didn't get caught.

This girl was so tired of people making fun of her because of what she looked like on the outside. They never really took the chance to see how nice of a person she was on the inside, but that didn't stop her from taking back her dignity. There were only a few people that really loved her for who she was and not for the way she looked or for the things she had.

I am the girl in this story. I'm the girl who got bullied everyday of my life. Sometimes it feels like I live in a tiny, empty hole where I feel like I'm a nobody and don't get the respect that I deserve.

My mother left me when I was born. My aunt took care of me, but had drinking problems. So I got put in DYFS. I still do not know my mother and I'm12. I'm now living with my foster mother, Doreen, and I've been with her for three years. I would like to thank Doreen for everything she has done for me and to tell her that I love her very much.

By Beverly Reed, 12
Belleville Middle School
Belleville, NJ

Fighting Back

Sixth grade is when it all started. You weren't in elementary school with all the people you had known since first grade, you were in middle school with different people. I was so nervous the teachers would be mean or the classes would be hard, I had no idea I was going to be bullied.

The first day of school we got our locker combinations and assigned to our homerooms. I was so excited to have my own locker and was hoping my friends were going to be in all of my classes but when I walked into homeroom I saw no familiar faces. I took a seat in the back of the room while all of the other people in my homeroom came in talking to one another. All the girls were gorgeous and I wasn't that pretty. I didn't wear Abercrombie or American Eagle like they did and I felt left out because I knew that none of that stuff would fit me or it was too expensive.

Anyways, one day I was walking down the hall and all I hear is laughing or someone whispering "Look at the fatty." I knew that they were talking about me because all the other girls around me were beautiful. I tried to hold it in and I tried not to cry but as soon as I got home that day I told my mom what had happened and cried. Things didn't seem to get any better. When I was in gym one day people were making fun of me because I couldn't run the mile fast enough. They would sit there and call me fat because they had to wait for me to finish. Every day it seemed like more and more people were starting to tease me so I would start to act like I was sick just to stay home. I couldn't even focus in class. I started to fail my classes. Everyone was telling me how great 6th grade was but I hated it.

To make things worse I had these 4 girls who lived right next to me and they thought it was fun to see who could send me home crying first. My mom was getting sick of me getting picked on everyday and said that I wouldn't be able to make it in 7th and 8th grade. She enrolled me in a school called Two Rivers Magnet Middle School. I wasn't too thrilled about this but she said it would be good for me. I hated her for this. There was no way I was going to go to some Magnet school.

When I got there I loved it right away. I made new friends who taught me to be tuff and stick up for myself. I stayed in that school for 2 years and by the time I left I knew I was ready for high school. Nobody was going to make fun of me now. Even if they did I knew how to stick up for myself. When I got there people didn't even remember me. I wasn't the same fatty 6th grader. I wasn't a dork anymore. Two Rivers Magnet Middle school changed my life.

By Alyssa Solak
Glastonbury High School
Glastonbury, CT

Learning Not to Bully Those From Other Cultures

Bully – that's the first word that popped into my head when I saw a new girl at my school being excluded from a game of Four Square at recess. She didn't understand the rules because she didn't understand English. She had not only recently moved to our area but she had moved from another country – Japan!! Her father worked at a foreign car manufacturing plant that had recently opened in our community and her family had moved half way around the world so they could have a better life in America.

I felt ashamed about what this poor girl must think of us Americans! I went to her, smiled and told her my name and asked her if I could sit with her. I'm not sure she understood but she did understand my smile and nodded her head yes. Our teacher had begun teaching us a few simple Japanese words before she arrived at our school so that we could try to communicate with her. I remembered one phrase she taught us was about meal time and I invited my new friend to eat lunch with me. I tried to make her feel like I wanted to be treated because I knew what it was like to be "the new kid." Although I didn't experience the language barrier she did, I did have to overcome the barrier of being accepted into already established circles of friends.

We have become good friends over the last three years and she speaks English very well. I have to admit I haven't made as much progress learning Japanese but that's OK because we accept each other as we are.

Many people are bullied for their race, clothes or even their religion. I think that most bullies just have low self esteem and it makes them feel important or popular. Most kids are usually bullied on the bus or just right after school or out of sight of an authority figure. The victim usually won't tell anyone because they are embarrassed or made to feel like they deserve being treated that way.

I think that bullying is wrong! I think every one should try to get along and try to understand that even if someone is different from them it may be because their families can't afford designer clothes or custom-made tennis shoes or they may just not understand our language or customs.

I think there should be video cameras at school so the principal and staff would know if there is a problem. If you are ever bullied or threatened, tell an adult you trust or speak with a school counselor or with the principal of your school about the problem. No one ever be allowed to be the victim of a bully.

By Kayla J. Rohaley, 11
Winfield Middle School
Scott Depot, WV

Words Hurt

As she walked down the stairs, she heard low murmurs behind her. She knew they were talking. They all talk, but they don't understand. They all make fun of her because of her weight, but they don't know the story behind it.

She gained twenty pounds over a very long and stressful summer. Her parents got divorced and her boyfriend broke up with her the same night her sister was arrested for drinking. She couldn't confide in anyone, so she relied on the food to comfort her. Usually an athletic person, she sat in front of the television shoving handfuls of junk food into her mouth. She tried to stop this habit, but she would become depressed without the food.

When she went back to school, no one recognized her. She was twenty pounds heavier, and three pant sizes bigger. The moment her friends saw her, they abandoned her, and wanted nothing to do with her. She heard rude comments all day long. And every night she would go home, lock herself in her room, and cry for hours straight.

Unfortunately, the bullying didn't stop there. In the halls, obnoxious teenage boys would knock her books down, and laugh at her when she bent down to pick them up. She tried out for soccer, thinking she could get into shape again, but she didn't make the team. People would constantly talk extremely loud when she was near. They would make fat jokes when she was around. She felt the kids enjoyed torturing her, she couldn't stand it anymore.

She talked to her parents, who talked to the guidance counselor. The counselor tried to set up a program against bullying, but it never followed through. And the bullying kept going. She had no friends, only enemies. People would knock her down and throw her papers everywhere. Even the observers did nothing to help. They just stood there and laughed so that they wouldn't be picked on.

She still relied on food. The bullying only made it worse, and she kept gaining weight. Her mom finally realized that her daughter was in danger. After many talks, they decided to move to a new district and start over. During the next summer, she lost weight and started over at new school. However, she was still scared for life. Her peers were so cruel that it forced her to move. She will never forget the pain she went through.

By Marissa Robinson, 15
Glastonbury High School
Glastonbury, CT

Would You Have Been Stronger?

Walking through the halls of high school is a life experience all should share. You become aware of what society is becoming and you observe others and choose whether you want to be like them or not. I know that in my high school the halls are tightly packed and you can't help but hear conversations as you pass by. Some are disturbing while others make you laugh uncontrollably. However, the particular one I am going to share was one that made me incredibly empty inside and overall made me a better person.

In school there is always that one person who seems to be picked on more than anyone else. Sometimes it's a girl and other times it's a guy. In this case it was a girl. When you hit high school you go two ways. You either are invincible or you are terrified. In the situation I am going to describe, the guys felt they were invincible.

As I was sitting in homeroom the Monday before the homecoming dance, I overheard the guys talking in class about who they were going to nominate for the homecoming ballot. I wasn't too surprised at the first three names but when they said the fourth my heart dropped. They had the nerve to nominate the girl (Susie) that they had been picking on since middle school but what was even worse is that they had all their buddies do the same thing so she would definitely make the cut. I felt so bad for her but what was I supposed to do, go up and say that she should drop out of the running? I couldn't ever do that to her so I just pretended I didn't hear a word they said.

Later, when they announced who had made the homecoming ballot, the second girl they named was Susie. When I saw her in the hallway she had a smile on her face and accepted her nomination for the ballot. I approached the guys and told them it was wrong to do what they were doing and that they should forget their plan. Of course they are guys and didn't listen to me. As a matter of fact they got angry at me for approaching them about it. After that I just took a back seat and let it play out.

Saturday, at the dance, Susie was wearing this hot pink and green dress that was something someone would wear in the eighties. I felt bad because she would have to be called up to the stage toward the middle of the night to be introduced as part of the homecoming court. The guys were still carrying out their plan and everything had a sour feeling about it. Susie's date didn't even go to our school. It was one of her church friends who no one at our school knew. Well, later on into the dance, the homecoming court nominees were introduced. The most popular girl in our school was named first and the guys whistled and girls cheered. Next was the captain of the girl's basketball team and the crowd cheered for her as well. Third was the speech and debate senior girl and finally was Susie. As soon as she began to walk up to the stage all the guys began to boo her. They did this until she reached the stairs to the stage. The look on Susie's face was one of embarrassment and humiliation. Even though the teachers were around and said a few things to the kids around them there really wasn't anything they could do to stop it.

The queen was announced and yes it was the most popular girl in our grade. Susie stepped down from the stage with tears in her eyes and I didn't see her the rest of the dance. What those boys put Susie through that entire week was wrong, a poor show of their character, and was something I hope never to witness again. As for my actions I am ashamed of myself. I could have said something to the teachers as this plan was brewing but instead I took a back seat and allowed someone to be hurt and humiliated in the process. As a senior this year, I have learned to embrace the people who are different and to never turn my head the other way when someone is being hurt. I hope others have learned from my mistake as well.

By Kerrie Haurin, 18
Canfield High School
Canfield, OH

Chapter: 2

Ask for Help

Write the names of a few people you can go to if you need help:

Everything You Need To Know About Bullying

In elementary school, kids were often made fun of or bullied. Although, everyone had their turn at getting hassled, some got it more than others. I saw things everyday, and some days certain kids dreaded coming to school.

Often I was the victim of the harassment, getting made fun of because of my last name. Over the years I have heard many different ways to say or spell my last name. These kids were relentless in making people feel awful about themselves. More than once I felt alone in the world with no one by my side. More often than not my "friends" wouldn't help, rather make the situation worse.

This continued into my middle school years. I thought that I would never be accepted by anyone other than my best friend, Chris. He was always by my side when I needed someone to hangout with or talk to. However, the problem was my self esteem. I didn't have the confidence in myself to do anything. Finally when I got the courage to do something, someone was there to knock me back down.

Once in high school, you have the chance to re-invent yourself, which is the best way to build your self esteem back up. The first year in high school was when I figured exactly what I needed to do; I learned that if you get one person to like you, the numbers quickly add up. However, if you didn't have a boyfriend/girlfriend, you were socially unacceptable. As a sophomore, I was still without a girlfriend, which is an esteem crusher for a fifteen year old guy.

I wasn't one who usually listens to what people think, but when the majority is making fun of you, it wears on your soul. Like an engine needs oil to run well, people need a boost for their self esteem to run well. Participate in something you excel at, you will feel better, you can change, you can conquer these feelings. Just remember that you have the strength, if you want it. Remember, character cannot be bought, sold or traded, only can it be earned; and things that make you feel awful about yourself don't destroy character, it strengthens it.

I would know, I lived though almost eleven years of bullying. This all stopped almost two years ago, in those two years I have succeeded in life. Live life to the fullest; don't let the details drag you down.

By Jon Lakoduk, 18
Minot High School - Magic City
Campus
Minot, ND

Bullies - A Problem Waiting to Be Solved

Many people have experienced a bully in their lives. They can be the victim, the bully, or the witness. It can happen face to face, on the Internet, in the classroom or on the school bus. Bullies can be your age or older. Bullies frighten or pick on people weaker than they are. It is not a very good experience. It could lower your self esteem and it could hurt feelings. You could be hurt physically or mentally. Bullies can be very mean, call you or your family names, start rumors about you, and sometimes embarrass you.

Last year, a group of friends that always stuck together began bullying me. They started to spread rumors about me and they wrote that I liked a boy that was mentally challenged on the board for the whole class to see. I kept erasing it and they kept writing it. I felt angry at them, upset, and alone. I did not like to go to that class because I knew that they would tease me. Sometimes I did not want to go to school, because I knew how I would feel when I saw them. I tried ignoring them at first, but it didn't really work. I thought about it at school and home. It affected my behavior and how I felt each day. I was not sure what to do. One day I was at gym class and they started bullying me again. I went to my gym teacher and told her what happened. She told me she would talk to them. She did speak with them, and they stopped teasing me. I did not feel that I had to avoid them anymore; I felt more comfortable going to class everyday. It was not on my mind anymore at home or at school. I told my parents what happened and they were upset. They told me that nobody has the right to make me feel bad about myself. They asked me if they could help, to let them know. I felt better knowing someone was on my side too. I did not feel so alone anymore.

Another time I witnessed bullies making fun of a boy on the bus. One child started talking mean about his family, and other children joined in. I know the family, and what they were saying is untrue and hurtful. I noticed the boy being bullied became very upset and angry. He became very defensive and started cursing at the children. I felt bad for him because I knew how he felt at that moment. He probably felt alone. It was them against him. The only way he seems to handle it is through anger and yelling back at them. I saw his personality change so he could defend himself. I don't think he told anyone about the incident. Now I know it is not good to keep it inside. It helps to tell a friend or any adult who can help.

I learned that people can be very mean sometimes even though you do not do anything to them. I did nothing to the girls who bullied me, and they started rumors about the boy and me. One of the girls used to be my friend. When she started "hanging out" with these other girls, her personality changed. She not only hurt me, but it was mean to make fun of the other boy too. Bullies make fun of kids for no reason. To them, it is a big joke. To the person being bullied, it causes many hurt feelings and intense emotions like anger, loneliness, embarrassment, and sadness.

I think students should be taught in school about bullies. It is important to make everyone aware that bullying is a big problem. Punishments should be given to the children who bully others. Bullies should be made aware of how they affect the people who are bullying. Nobody has the right to make other people feel bad about themselves. I also think the victims of bullies should know that they are not alone, and that there are people who can help them. They have to not be afraid and tell an adult what is going on. It is not healthy to hold it all inside. I think there should not be any more bullying! Bullying is not good!

Many people have experienced a bully at least once in their lives. It may have happened to them, they may see it happen to someone else, or they may even be the person bullying. There are many ways to be bullied, but the results are usually the same. People get hurt mentally or physically. People should not make other people feel frightened or insecure. I think if more people are made aware of the problem, we can put an end to bullying. I also think it is important that people say that they are being bullied. They should not keep it to themselves. They can get help from someone because they are not alone.

By Kathryn A. Costidius, 12
Smithtown Middle School
Saint James, NY

Bully, Are You One?

The topic I am going to talk about is bullies. Have you ever been bullied before, or have you bullied someone? I have been bullied before and it's not a good thing. When I think of the word bully, I think of a really mean person. The bully always bosses people around and tells them what to do. Bullies also make fun of people, like the way they dress or look.

One of my classmates at school always gets made fun of by how short she is and also because she has crooked teeth. She always feels so bad and stupid and she never wants to show her face in school. At lunch she always sits alone because she has no friends to laugh with, talk to, or to tell secrets to. So one day my friend and I went up to her and asked if she would be our friend. She looked up from her lunch tray and smiled at us and said, "Yes". My friend and I felt so happy that she was happy and now had two great friends. Ever since that day we asked her to be our friend, she has been a lot happier. Finally, the bully stopped bullying her and everyone was so happy.

Here is a short poem about bullying:

B-Bad person
U-Ugly
L-Low self-esteem
L-Liked by other bullies
Y-You are mean to people.

My action plan is if a bully was bullying me I would tell an adult. If a bully kept bullying me every day, I would tell a teacher or my parents.

My conclusion of the story would be to treat people the way you would want to be treated. If a bully is mean to you, just walk away.

By Kelsey Mullins, 12
Valley View Middle School
Germantown, OH

Dear Diary

December 4, 2004

Dear Diary, today was awful because my friend Reagan was being bullied and I had no clue what to do to help her. It all started when we were in gym class and to let you know Reagan isn't the most athletic girl in the world. So anyways, we were running ladders and Natasha, a popular athletic girl, started making fun of Reagan by saying stuff like, "Slowpoke," "Get out of my way clumsy." I saw Natasha saying this stuff to Reagan but I didn't say anything because I didn't think that the name calling that she said was bad. All she was saying was slowpoke and stuff like that. Well, let's see if tomorrow is better. Goodnight diary.

December 5, 2004

Dear Diary, so much for the "let's see if tomorrow is any better." Guess what, the name-calling got worse. Today Natasha was cursing, running into Reagan and knocking down all of her stuff, pushing her into her locker, and more. That's when I stepped in. I thought that Natasha was

going way over the line. When we were in athletics I saw
Natasha pushing Reagan around. So I walked up and said,
"Stop Natasha. This is going way over the line now. What
has Reagan ever done to you to deserve this?" Natasha then
yelled in my face, "You better get out of this because it is
none of your business." I couldn't believe that she said
that! So when I got enough courage I stepped up to her and
said, "It's my business because she is my friend and friends
are suppose to stand up for each other." By then Natasha
was really mad, she started pushing me around, and calling
me names. Did I do the right thing diary?

December 10, 2004

Dear Diary, so today in the hallway Reagan I were walking together to go to our 3rd period class and along the way
Natasha and all of her friends came by and stopped right in
front of us. We told them to move and we tried to work our
way around them but they kept us from going to our class.
I then said, "Natasha please move. We are trying to go to
class." Then Natasha said that she was going to keep us
from going to class so that we would be late. The thing that
bothers me is she couldn't be late because she was going to
work in the office and the office people always let her get
away with being late. So finally, when she let us go we ran
to class and still ended up being late. So Reagan and I got
detentions! How wonderful. Not.

December 12, 2004

Dear Diary, today Reagan and I went to early morning
detention and our mothers were upset with us. I tried to tell
my mom that it wasn't our fault but she didn't want to lis-

ten to me at that moment. So we went into the detention room and we had to straighten book shelves, vacuum the floors, and then do work. It was terrible and I never want to go to detention again!

December 17, 2004

Dear Diary, Reagan and I both decided that we had enough of Natasha so we went and told our mothers. They asked us why we didn't tell them earlier and we didn't answer. Now that I think about it I really have no clue why we didn't tell them because it really hurt to be cussed at and to be pushed around. I hated seeing her and was so scared of what she was going to do to me next. If this had gone on for very much longer I think that I would want to transfer schools because of her. Well, she has stopped now and I like going to school to be with Reagan and not having to worry about Natasha anymore. Thanks Diary for being there for me!

By Brittany M. Folsom, 13
Forney Middle School
Forney, TX

What is a Bully?

A bully is a person who orders, or bosses people around. It is a person who doesn't care of the other person's feeling. It is a person who doesn't care if the other person gets hurt. It is a person that makes you think and believe that you are worthless, and makes fun of your physical features. Most of all, [a bully] is a person that changes the way you act, and the way you think about yourself when you look at yourself in the mirror. It is a person that obligates you to do something that you are not happy in doing. It is a person that makes you go home and cry alone, not able to tell your parents, brothers, sisters, cousins, or anyone because you are too scared.

How do I know how it feels? How do I know the horrible feeling and the pain that person feels? How? It is because it really happened to me. It is a really tormenting thing. You can't sleep because you have nightmares. In school you can't really think of math problems, concentrate on your reading, or learn because you are thinking that the person who is bothering you and picking on you is waiting for you in the hallway. To embarrass you, to tell you to do stuff, to call you names, to makes fun of your love ones. All you can do is just stay quiet and swallow that, like it never happened. That's what I did, which I now understand you shouldn't do. It will bother you even more, if you swallow it and never say anything to anyone.

I tried telling my mom, but I couldn't. I couldn't make her stress, or worry about me. She had a lot of stuff going on. Even though she told me one night that if I had a problem to come to her or my dad anytime. I didn't want them to worry. I couldn't tell the teacher or the vice principal, because if the person who was bothering me gets ISS or OSS I knew he was going to be after me. So I didn't know what to do. All I did was after school I would walk to my house and into my room. I would lock my door and lay down in my bed and begin to cry.

In the morning before I would go to school I would go and hug my mom and give her a kiss on her cheeks. It felt so good. My heart is close to hers. It was like saying "It's okay my son. I am here for you. I will protect you." I felt so warm and [with] love in my heart. Until it was time, time for me to say good-bye and head to school. I felt as if I only went to school to get tormented. I was so scared especially walking through those doors [that] my heart was pumping faster and faster. I knew he was going to appear in front of me. He was going to tell me to do something inappropriate, or tell me to give him the money that my mom gave to me to give my dad for my brother's medicine.

Walking in the hallway was so terrifying. My heart was pumping faster and faster. When I was one room away from my class, he appeared to me and said to give him money. In my head I asked myself if I should give him my brother's medicine money or tell him "no". I reached into my pocket and gave him in the money. I ran to my class and sat in my seat with head down, my forehead laying in the edge of the desk. I began to cry. "Now, what am I going to do?"

"My little brother is sick. What am I going to do?" After school I wondered about how I was going to tell my dad I didn't have the money for my brother's medicine.

When my father arrived to pick me up, I told him that I lost the money. I told him that I was very sorry. "Son, how can you be irresponsible!" He responded. "I'm sorry," I replied. I felt so bad not only for giving the money to the person who picks on me but also because I lied to my father. I shouldn't have given it to him. On the way to the pharmacy I began to cry, without my father noticing I wiped my tears off my face. When we got there, my father suggested I'd stay in the car because it was too cold and he didn't wanted me to be sick.

When my father came back to the car, we left for home so my brother could take the medicine. When we got home, I went directly to my room and began to do my homework. When I finished my work, I turned on my T.V. and started to watch my favorite cartoons, the Rugrats. Then I realized that I hadn't been paying any attention to my little brother, so I stood up and headed to my brother's room. Peeking through the open door I saw my little brother coughing, and my mom next to him. I changed my mind about going in and decided not to go in. I felt so bad. I felt even worse knowing I needed to go to school in the morning. I was so stressed out worrying about a lot of things especially thinking of what is going to happen to me in school.

In the morning when I went to school, I found out that the guy who was tormenting me, bothering me, bossing me around, was moving to another state. When I found that out I couldn't believe it until my favorite teacher told me it was true. I was so happy. Now, nobody is going to boss me around, embarrass me in front of my friends, tell me to give him my money. I have never seen him since the day he told me to give him my brother's medicine money. Now, all I remember is that I have been picked on and bossed around since I was in fifth grade until eighth grade.

This really hurt me and changed the way I was but it taught me a lesson. It taught me that if something is bothering me to tell someone. It is a bad idea if you keep it in yourself and don't say anything to anyone. All that does is hurt you even more. Remember a bully's goal is to boss you around, make you do stuff for them, but most of all is change the way you are and think about yourself. That is why you should stand up for yourself. Don't resolve problems with fists, though, resolve it by talking to the person or talking to someone that will do something about it like your teachers, vice principal, etc.

Remember don't let anyone put you down because all that does is make you see someone else in the mirror and not you later in life.

By Juan Munoz, 15
Perth Amboy High School
Perth Amboy, NJ

Bullying the New Kid

When I was younger, I used to get bullied a lot. I still don't know why it happened to me; I was a quiet kid who kept to herself. I wouldn't even talk to people other than my family and friends unless they talked to me first.

I remember hating to go to school because I always got bullied. I worried about it so much, the stress made me sick. In fact, when I was in fourth grade, the fear of being bullied made me sick enough to miss 14 days of school.

Usually it was just one girl who decided she hated me and was going to do everything in her power to make my life miserable from the moment she first saw me, before any words were exchanged. She tormented me by herself, but when she was with her group of friends, it was the worst. Most of them just stood there watching, but a few would come in after something the biggest bully said and say something rude, and the whole group would start laughing.

I can't even remember how many times I came home in tears. I tried to hide it from my mom for a few months, by saying I fell down on the way home or something like that. After a while, she caught on that something was happening at school and made me tell her what it was.

She called the school principal, and the next day there I sat next to the bully telling my side of the story to the principal. I was so nervous sitting next her and afraid that she was going to lie and say I did something cruel to her, I couldn't help but cry. I'm amazed the principal could even understand me, I was crying so hard.

The bully didn't lie or try to twist the story, and she admitted that she was going out of her way to make my life a living nightmare. The principal called her parents and sent me out to recess.

I was so relieved to finally be rid of the constant teasing, I skipped all the way home from school that afternoon. When my mom asked me how things went at school that day, I replied "Great! That girl is finally going to get off of my back!" I slept easy that night for the first time since that school year began.

But I was wrong. After a couple of weeks, the bully seemed to forget all about the principal's little chat with her parents, and the bullying got worse. Now not only did she tease me mercilessly, but every time she passed my desk she knocked something off of it. Within a few days, she began to spread rumors about me; all of which were untrue.

After telling her to stop repeatedly, I told my mom the bullying had not ceased, but instead had escalated. My mom called the principal again, then the bully and I both sat next to each other in the principal's office the next day. This time the principal was really hard on her, saying that if she didn't stop she would get suspended. Her parents must have punished her, because finally the bullying stopped.

I was ecstatic! As the weeks turned into months, she left me alone. That is, until one day.

On this particular day, though, she didn't approach me in a threatening manner. In fact, she handed me an apology card and begged my forgiveness. She said she thought about what she put me through, and realized it was not a cool thing to do. She even wanted to become my friend, and I accepted on a trial basis.

She kept being nice to me, and so did other friends. Eventually we became the best of friends, having sleep-overs every weekend.

It just goes to show that everyone has a lot more fun when nobody is bullied and everyone just accepts everyone as they are. It is our uniqueness, after all, that makes life truly interesting.

By Jamie Leigh Jutrzonka, 14
Oak Creek East Middle School
Manitowoc, WI

Billy the Bulldog ("The Class Bully")

It was my fourth grade year in school at Norwood Elementary. There was a new student in our class. His name was Jack. Jack was very quiet and he did not socialize very well with the other students. He was a special needs student. Some of the children in the classroom made fun of him when he talked. Jack couldn't help it though. He needed extra help with talking, writing, and communicating with people. I felt sorry for Jack. I wanted to be his friend.

Then there is Billy. I have been in school with Billy since kindergarten. His nickname is "Billy the Bulldog". He likes to take your lunch money and your snack that you have brought from home to eat in the bus room. He even threatens to beat you up if you don't give him your money. One time I saw him steal my neighbor's homework and claimed for his own. He is ruthless. I try to stay clear of him. I guess because I'm a girl he doesn't bother me much. But that's not the story for Jack. Since Jack is different Billy zeroed in on him.

For several weeks Billy would take Jack's lunch money and Jack never got to eat. I tried to tell Jack he needs to tell the teacher, but Jack was too afraid. He said that Billy would beat him up if he told anyone. Next, Billy would sit next to Jack on the bus and he would pinch Jack until it made red marks on his arm. I guess when Jack's mother asked him about the marks he said that he did it to himself. I figure his mother believed him since he did have some problems. This worried me. How could I convince Jack to talk to someone about Billy? This was not right to be treated so badly.

I made a decision that if Jack wasn't going to tell someone that I would. I didn't want Jack to get in trouble with Billy, but this has gone too far. I built up my courage and I talked with Mrs. Peters, our teacher. She was very upset. She had Billy sent to the principal's office and his parents called. I guess Billy's parents were very upset with him. Billy was made to apologize and as far as I know, he has not bothered Jack since. Now I'm so happy to see Jack eat his lunch. Jack has made some new friends and just yesterday Jack read a whole page in front of the class.

By Megan E. Fox, 11
Bridgeport Middle School
Bridgeport, WV

Bullying the Quiet Kid

Bullying is a cruel act because it creates low self-esteem, fear, and loneliness in the person being bullied. Low self-esteem affects our confidence. We need confidence to do well in our lives. Of course we know fear makes us afraid to try new things. No one wants to be lonely. We need to be able to depend on each other. There is no room for a bully when we stick together.

Webster's dictionary defines a bully as a person usually cruel to others who are weaker. Bullying happens in almost every school and playground and even as adults they experience this cruel, humiliating act. Bullies tend to pick on smaller or weaker kids just to show their dominance. Dominance meaning authority or control.

Bullying to me is trying to control someone, thinking they may be popular or tough and everyone wanting to be around them. What they may not understand unless it has happened to them is how it makes the person being bullied feel. I have been there before. It made me feel sick and I found myself making excuses to my parents just so that I could stay home and not deal with my bully. I was unhappy and I felt alone. Around the time this was happening to me, by luck my school passed out a brochure, and guess what? Bullying was the topic. This was great. It allowed me to confide in my parents about what was happening to me at school. I was able to overcome my fears. We decided to pass this on to my favorite bully and I guess it helped him too. Things are fine now and we have become friends.

I realized I wasn't the problem, the bully was. We need to recognize this act of hurt and let others know this is not O.K. My grandmother always says "treat others the way you expect to be treated" and who knows, this bully may have been a victim himself.

As a community, school or family we need to stand together and stop bullying. It truly is an ugly word and no one wants to be bullied or be a bully. But think about this; are you a bully or have you ever bullied someone else? If your answer is yes, please find other ways to feel good about yourself. This isn't the way to get your name in the school yearbook for most popular. Let's find a way together to put an end to bullying.

I'm thankful that my school and my family were there for me. This brochure wasn't just another pamphlet that was sent home in my folder to be thrown away but a very important reminder that I was able to pass on and possibly help someone else. Thank you.

By Zachary Jordan Teter, 11
Bridgeport Middle School
Bridgeport, WV

Look Around That Corner

Have you ever been bullied? Have you ever had that feeling in your stomach that you knew as soon as you turned that corner, that bully would be sitting there? That feeling of distraught and sadness just knowing everyday you wake up, that bully will, once again, find delight in torturing you in every possible way they can think of?

Last year, I experienced this kind of torment for quite a long time. It would happen almost everyday, all day. They would try to find just the right time to either ridicule me or put me down (emotionally) in every single way they thought of. Whether it was because I made the highest grade in class, or because I won the big contest at school. It could have even been the fact that I got a new backpack over the weekend. Sometimes you could tell that every word coming from those girls' mouths was pure jealousy.

Being the victim of this type of situation taught me a lot. I have realized that you can quickly learn who your true friends are. I have learned through experience that teachers can totally change this situation around. I had one teacher that truly turned my situation upside down. She helped me get out my feelings and understand why someone would have the desire to bully someone like me.

When I was faced with this, I simply took it in and tried to ignore them as much as possible. I tried to NOT take matters into my own hands and let someone with authority handle it. The girls involved with this got pleasure seeing me in pain and misery. I simply prayed for them in a way that they could see their hateful actions.

Since being in that situation, I now make sure to watch out and be aware of the people around me. I have tried to be kind and show a great example for people this year. I have been watching out for bullies and I hate to see people being tormented by them. I continually see bullies walking down the hall just after they crushed someone emotionally. I can only pray that one day they realize what their actions have caused and that someday they see The Light.

by Shae Goldston, 13
Forney Middle School
Forney, TX

Hurting Someone's Feelings is Worse Than What You Think

What is the worst thing that could happen to a kid in school? To some, it would be bad grades and to others it would be getting in trouble with the teacher, but to most kids, it's getting bullied by other people. There have been a lot of reports about bullying in school. I have been bullied, have seen some being bullied, and have been a bully myself without even knowing I was one. We tend to forget what's good or bad and bully someone for our own pleasure, not caring about the victim's emotions.

Some of my friends and I used to make fun of people because of how they looked or acted. We would usually laugh about someone and share stories about their behavior we found peculiar. Sometimes, we even laughed right in front of them, usually when they were passing us or when we were passing them. We never thought they ever cared about what we said because they never said or did anything to make us stop.

I realized what I did was wrong after entering a new school in fifth grade. It happened around September 2002 and school just started. I arrived in the United States about four months ago, but it was my first time starting school here, so I felt quite excited to finally meet people of a different race. When the teacher introduced me to the class, most of them were eager to help me out if I was confused with something. Everyone was fine with me and I thought that my new school life was going to be fine.

After my first class, this girl near me suddenly told me that she hated me, called me names, and said that I should stay away from her. Being my second day, I had no idea what I did wrong, so I just ignored her hoping she'll get over it. She did not stop calling me names and for several days I had to constantly endure the mean remarks still hoping that she would stop later on. I did stay away from her because I didn't want to be in an argument with her. I never thought of telling the teacher about it that early of the year because I thought I could probably handle it myself. I probably wouldn't have felt bad if I had done something to make her hate me, but I didn't and soon, I thought that she was picking on me because I was new and that I was probably different from the rest of them.

To my dismay, she didn't cease her comments about me. One day, I just had enough and could not stop myself from telling the teachers. They talked to me and to the girl about it individually and told her to stop calling me names. Later that day, I kind of regretted telling the teachers about what happened, thinking she might take this badly and pick on me more. The next day, I was surprised when she greeted me happily as if we were long-time friends. We soon became friends and she hasn't picked on me since.

Everyone should do something to stop bullying. The victims and the witnesses should tell an adult about bullying and not try to handle it by themselves. Teachers and other adults should look for ways to at least lessen the bullying incidents in schools. They should make groups or clubs where they can share their experiences and make kids feel good about themselves. They should build the children's confidence by advising them about what to do and what not to do when encountering a bully. Teachers and parents should also confront the bullies and talk to them and try to solve out their problems.

After my experience with a bully, I realized that if you call someone names, they get emotionally hurt and this might affect them in the future. Unlike physical harm, emotional pain might have lasting effects such as low self-esteem. Some bullies experience these feelings too and they try to bring out their anger by inflicting the same feelings to other people. Though they have problems of their own, they shouldn't bully others just to relieve themselves. Everyone, including the bullies, should tell someone about these problems because it would be an easier burden to carry if you have someone to help you with it.

By Jeremy B. Buhain, 13
Belleville Middle School
Belleville, NJ

Character Lessons

What character traits does a bully
need to learn?

The Act of Kindness

Have you ever been bullied or have bullied someone else? I have seen a lot of people bullying and being bullied in high school. I myself have also been bullied.

One time this kid was being really mean. He would always push me, call me names, and always insult me. He would be unkind to me daily without fail. He would call me some names that would hurt really bad and was embarrassing, and it was hard for me to forget those names. The really sad thing was I didn't know why he would always pick on me. I had never done anything to him before. I'm not sure if he did it just because he was one of the shortest people in my grade or what the reason was, but I do know that the bullying made me feel really sad and depressed, and not very good about myself. He would do it in front of my friends and other people at school in the halls.

However, I just couldn't let him keep bullying me. So I had to do something, but what? I kept thinking and thinking of what to do. I couldn't be mean back to him because that would make me no better than him. I definitely did not want to stoop down to his level. All that would do is make me a bully also and that is exactly what I was trying to get rid of. So how do you overcome bullying by not being a bully? I thought about this for a long time. Then it hit me with great excitement. Kindness, all I need to do is be kind!

Even though it might not work I was going to try to kill him with kindness. Instead of avoiding him, I just acted like he was my friend. Whenever I would see him I would always compliment him, say "Hi" and treat him nicely. At first the process was slow because he would still make fun of me and be rude but I at least felt better about myself. Then after a month it started to work but not quite how I expected because it was the people around him that started to make the change. His friends would always give him a hard time for being mean to me because I was always friendly to all of them and nice. After about a month he was never mean to me again and his friends stopped giving him a hard time too.

Although we never became friends we also never said bad things about each other and he to started to say "Hi" when he saw me at school. I feel that although he was mean to me in the beginning, in the end I had been so kind that not only did I feel better about myself, he felt good about himself too. Therefore he didn't have to degrade other people to make him feel good about himself. I learned that having a good character about you and showing respect for others regardless of the situation is really cool!

By Tyson Bybee, 15
Highland High School
Pocatello, ID

Emotional Buildup

Scared, embarrassed, sad, mad, depressed, intimidated. These are all the words that come to my mind when I think about a girl I knew. She was like a best friend to me. This girl used to be picked on a lot. It started in the fourth grade. When she got to her school, she forgot where she had to go, she asked the nearest girl. She had no idea that this girl would change her fourth grade life.

The week after, the girl had made new friends. The group of friends started off well, but after awhile, the group didn't like this girl anymore. When the girl went to go talk to them they would move away. When she wore a nice shirt they would say that's an ugly shirt. If they didn't like her hairstyle they would make fun her. They even spread [things] that were not true. "Why are they doing this to me? Why don't I tell someone? I can't. They could hurt me, besides no one would understand," the girl would think.

This girl had just about had it, but what was she supposed to do? She was scared of them. So she coped with it and her feelings started to build up inside. She would yell at her remaining friends for what other people had done to her. She herself had become a bully.

I know this because that girl was me. It wasn't until a good friend told me that I had changed, and that they didn't like the new "me." After a while I changed and ignored those girls who bullied me.

I can remember this part of my life vividly for many reasons. First off, this was a tough and scary time for me, and I thought there was no one else to turn to. As I grew older I found out that there were many people out there feeling the same way I felt.

Sometimes I wish if I could turn back time. I realized that one of my good friends had been going through the same exact thing. Those friends that stood with me are still with me today. I will always remember what happened to me in fourth grade.

Here's my message to all the bullies:

> I may dress differently than you.
> I may not look like you.
> I may act differently than you,
> but we are actually the same.
> We both breathe air from the trees
> and sometimes we want to fall to our knees
> crying with tears of sadness.
> You can bully me all you want
> but it's not a thing to flaunt
> or be proud of because you can make me cry.
> Sometimes I know
> but you won't let it show
> that you sometimes enjoy what you do.
> But what you keep inside
> is something you try to hide
> but I can see right through.

Inside you are truly blue
insecure, sad, afraid or mad
because of that you make others feel bad,
but beyond that I see a light
that doesn't shine very bright.
With a little help and a good friend
you could be a better person till the end.

By Samantha Soto, 13
Belleville Middle School
Belleville, NJ

Better Than Cute

I have a neighbor and longtime friend with Downs Syndrome. He and I have known one another since we were in pre-school. We would go to each other's birthday parties and visit each other's houses to play with the rest of the neighborhood kids. On Halloween, all of us would go trick-or-treating together, and when Easter rolled around, we would attend the neighborhood Easter-egg hunt. I must say that my friend has to be one of the friendliest and outgoing people that I have ever met.

As students exit the school bus, he will give each person a high-five and say goodbye. In the hallways, he says hello to everyone and makes sure he knows everyone's names. Never has there been a time that I have seen him in an angry mood or mad at anyone. When other people call him "cute" or "special" because of his disabilities it constantly angers me. I never feel like I have to stand up for him because he is extremely capable of defending himself. He just never seems to be minded by anything. The problem to me is that he was talked about without his knowing. It is as if he was a baby when people called him cute, in actuality, he is turning sixteen in April, and is probably the oldest student in our grade.

He has come a long way and his disability has never blocked his path. When he would say hello to one girl in the hallways, or at lunch, she would say hi and once he left she would start to make fun of him. She said how she was so annoyed that he would come up to her and bother her while she was eating, or that he would come up to her while she was talking with her friends, who obviously seemed more important to her. Every time I would see him courageously go up to her and her group of friends, she would mockingly say "hi" and laugh once he left. I couldn't stand it.

I'm pretty sure he has now realized that she is not worthy of his friendliness. I had never been brave enough to ever go up to her and say something, but if it continued, I'm sure I would. To this day, people still call him "cute", and I follow with "Cute? .... Cute? He's older than you!"

Never has my friend been bothered by people's rudeness, because he doesn't let it get to him. Nothing ever gets to him, he never stoops to the level of those girls. He is the bigger one. No matter what disability he has, I think he is a stronger person than anyone who makes fun of him.

By Nicole McDermott, 14
Glastonbury High School
Glastonbury, CT

Bullying from an Aspergian Perspective

When I was in fourth grade, I spent the year in two different schools. The first was one that I had been attending since kindergarten. It was an average school. It was not too difficult, but it was challenging. I had many friends there. I was well known for my encyclopedic knowledge.

Then, halfway through the year, my mother persuaded me to transfer to the school at which she taught. I went there for a day to survey it. The students seemed nice, so I agreed to go. It was fine for the first few days.

We were then given an assignment which involved speaking in front of the class. I have Asperger's Syndrome, which makes public speaking difficult for me. At my former school, everyone somehow realized and respected that, even though I had never discussed it with them. Here, however, nobody seemed to be the least bit concerned.

Furthermore, I was the subject of much psychological bullying. My classmates would often poke fun at my inherent shyness. I turned to the teacher for assistance. She merely told me to ignore them. This failed, as they were the only people I could associate with at the time.

They continued with their insults. I tried to ignore them, but to no avail. It was as though they were following me everywhere for the sole purpose of making me feel inferior. This time, I told my mother. She gave the exact same advice as my teacher had. I began to feel more and more isolated as time passed. It was as though everyone had turned against me. This made me feel belligerent.

Times did improve slightly. A few of my classmates began calling me their friend. This boosted my morale, and I was able to ignore the taunting for a while. However, my new-found friends rarely supported me in my struggle against the neurotypicals. I was too naïve to realize this at the time.

The year ended at long last. I told my mother that I wanted to go back to my old school. She did not understand, but she agreed. I was finally happy again. I later realized that I could harness my emotions and even eliminate them entirely. This has made me a much more contented person.

One of my friends from middle school attends high school with these so-called "friends" from elementary school. He informed me that they actually despised me. However, this does not bother me in the least.

by Garrett Maner, 15
Capital High School
Charleston, WV

Bullying For the Cause

At one point in life, everyone has been exposed to bullying. Either they were the victim, the bully, or just a witness. Most people look at bullying as a mean person pushing around an innocent person. Perhaps, though, it could sometimes be just the opposite.

By this I mean a person pressuring another with a good intent. Most people would consider this positive peer pressure, but there is a point where peer pressure can turn into bullying. In young adults it happens quite often when trying to prove a point or discourage a bad behavior. An example of this would be if a person's behavior were offending somebody. One person might say something and, whether they stop or not, more people join in scalding that person. Pretty soon an entire crowd has ganged up on that one person for something they did. This shows that the victim of bullying does not and isn't always totally innocent. However, it still makes bullying wrong. How do we draw the line between standing up for yourself and being a bully? It is one thing to defend your rights and beliefs, but it is another to victimize those who challenge those rights and beliefs. As soon as the other person begins to feel threatened of being alienated, it has become bullying. This can come about by becoming overly defensive (which can trigger a fight-or-flight thought process) or when more than one person is rebuking another.

If, in fact, this were true about bullying, then I would have to admit to being a bully on one or more occasions. This is because, at times, I get defensive. I can recall a time when I was with a group of people at a basketball game. One girl took off her sweatshirt only to have a revealing top on. This made us all feel very uncomfortable, especially the young men. Instead of just asking her to please cover up, we made discreet efforts to try to make her feel uncomfortable with what she was wearing. I was the one to start it by coughing under my breath, "Modesty!" Someone else followed by expressing how hard it was for her to find a dress for the dance that was appropriate. The girl took a hint, but didn't seem to care. She answered by saying that her top wasn't very appropriate, but at least it was cute and attractive. So finally one of the boys told her that he didn't like the view he had and asked her to put her sweatshirt back on. She did. However, as if that wasn't enough, we still continued to basically try to shame her of her actions with the comments we made.

Now I realize that we were making her feel uncomfortable and alienated. She probably won't display her revealing attire to us anymore; however, she won't hang around us anymore either. She has her own free will, and it was not our place to try to take that away from her. If any of us were offended by her actions, one of us simply needed to politely express that and leave the rest up to her. I try to remember that every time a similar situation arises. I respect that person's freedom of choice after I politely voice my opinion or concern.

The act of bullying is not always the product of ill intent, but can sometimes be from good. Too easily does standing up for what's right turn into battering the offender. Although some good can come from this "positive peer-pressure," the person being pressured might be feeling forced to do or say something and often times feel ganged up on for not being good enough. We need to realize that it is not always our responsibility to try to improve or change others. We all have our own freedom of choice to be who we want to be. We, as a whole, need to draw the line between defending and offending so that we don't go from being the Good Samaritan to a plain bully.

By Stephanie Rolz, 16
Highland High School
Pocatello, ID

Skin Deep

"Sticks and stones may break my bones, but names will never hurt me." Some of us go by that philosophy, while others beg to differ. I used to believe those words. Eminem once spoke such crimson flames of truth in his single, "Like Toy Soldiers": *"There used to be a time when you could just say a rhyme and wouldn't have to worry about one of your people dying."*

Have you ever wished you could go back and change things? I admit I've been a part of bullying. I've jumped on the bandwagon to fit in at other people's expenses. Never once had I thought words could be so cruel, until I, myself experienced the agony and pain.

"What goes around comes around." My friends decided one day to play a joke on me, by excluding me and verbally playing with my emotions. They pushed me away from any social opportunity and called me names. Being an insecure person, I took their comments seriously. I believe that it's normal at times to feel worthless, but when someone else says it; it's like a big slap in the face. You feel because those words have come out of someone else's mouth, it must be true and there is no way to change it.

I felt as if I wanted to lock myself away from the world, never to be seen again. Despite the fact that I was suffering inside, I decided to laugh it off like it was no big deal instead of actually telling my friends that it wasn't right. Like Linkin Park said in their song, "Easier To Run": *"wounds so deep, they never show, they never go away, like moving pictures in my head, for years and years they've played."* This experience still eats away at me each and every time I look back.

My sixth grade teacher once said, "You're not sorry for what you did, you're sorry because you got caught." Now because of my previous experience, I can in fact say with all my heart; I am sorry if I've ever hurt someone else with my words. I've learned that you can't erase the past, so learn from your mistakes. Bullying isn't always about the bruises and scars on the outside; it is truly more than skin deep.

> Shelter me with warmth
> And wipe away my tears
> Come take me away
> To anywhere, but here.
> Cause, the days are now long
> And the air is still cold
> The nights are lonely
> With no one there to hold.
> I'll swallow my breath
> And hope to survive
> This daily routine
> I shall endure to thrive.
> This home now feels distant
> Yet I've been here before
> These broken memories
> Will have me striving for more.
> I've moved on since then,

But the feeling will stay
And all I've got left
Is to sit here and pray.
There's no use forgetting
Or making any excuse
Forever down I'll be
I'm a child of your abuse.

By Tram Dao, 13
Belleville Middle School
Belleville, NJ

Bravery vs. Bullying

Discrimination, harassment, intimidation, bullying, call it what you want to. Bottom line is almost everyone has experienced some form of this abuse. Not to mention, the same people have watched someone be abused and have done nothing about it. This must change.

America is "The Land of Freedom" so why are so many United States citizens verbally and physically abused daily? They say it takes a village to raise a child. In my opinion, it going to take a lot more than a village to stop this crime. Yes, I mean crime; a crime that many times goes unpunished or even worse, accepted.

Have you ever been scared to go to school or go to the bathroom or walk in the halls of your school? Have you ever witnessed someone being physically beat up or taken to jail from your school? I have. Even though I was not the direct target, I've witnessed it and have been too afraid to do anything about it. Doesn't that make me just as guilty as the person literally doing it?

How can we stop this exploitation? Have you heard the phrase "United We Stand"? I want to try to make a difference in someone's life.

I know what it is going to take – BRAVERY.

I firmly believe that I should start with developing character in elementary school aged children. Students of Character is a program that is designed to instill six pillars of character education into children at a young age so they will carry out these traits as they grow up to be adults. I will focus on respect, responsibility, citizenship, caring, trustworthiness and fairness. I truly believe building these traits in people will band bullying. My plan is to utilize my after school time to visit elementary campuses, student groups; such as girl and boy scouts, dance studios, and sports groups. I'm creating real life situational lessons that include all children to identify with and assist them in making the right choices.

I envision strong character traits as being prerequisites for students participating in extracurricular activities. I have spoken with the Facilitator of Character Development for our district and she has shared my philosophy and ideas with the Humble ISD Superintendent and he is in favor of this initiative.

It is a human trait to want to be accepted. Research shows that a bully suffers too. They are not only hurting inside, but as they get older many fail to keep jobs or have positive interpersonal relationships, so many are convicted of crimes by the age of twenty-four.

Having strong character is a LIFE skill and is imperative in creating a safer nation. Please consider joining me and model good character. Remember, the person that is bullying you is really hurting inside. This vicious cycle must stop.

I've always been somewhat shy and quiet so this is going to take a lot of bravery for me to accomplish this endeavor. If everyone could find it in their heart to strive to possess this type of bravery, good character would prevail.

Compromises could be reached among people of differing cultures and beliefs. I'm ready for the challenge. Are you?

By Carlee Gabrisch, 16
Humble High School
Humble, TX

My Battle with a Bully

Most likely, everyone has had a bully in their past. Some use their experiences to grow as an individual, while others hold them against their oppressor. Whenever I had a bully, I forgave them as quickly as possible, but some situations were harder than others. I decided to try to be the bigger person and be as much unlike them as possible. Hopefully I made a good impact on someone else's life, because it was one of the only ways that I could overcome my anger. Bullies can be conquered; all it takes is a little courage, patience, and forgiveness.

While growing up, I've always been accepted but was by no means the top of the social food chain. The seventh grade was one of the worst years due to a boy I'll call Craig. One of Craig's main problems was that he yearned for attention. He knew practically every cuss word in the book. Craig's main victims were girls like me who were timid and whose feelings could be hurt easily. When he knew that I fell under this category, he didn't waste any time trying to make me as miserable as possible.

When my experiences with Craig began, I had been laying out our class's reading logs and handed his to him. The idea that I would even touch his belongings obviously disgusted him to no end, and he let me know it, along with a string of unpleasant words. I tried to stay calm, but I was heartbroken that anyone would do that to me and I began to cry. I shouldn't have done this because it showed him he could get under my skin very easily, so the torture continued until my parents and I had the principal get involved. After the principal talked with each of us, Craig eventually became less of a tormenter. Seventh grade ended, and I haven't seen him since.

Because of these experiences, I strongly believe that people need to think before they speak or act to. If they disregard the differences between their enemies, then their enemies could become friends. I wish that people would try to consider everyone as their equal instead of thinking that they are better than everyone around them. If everyone had that attitude, then there would probably be less violence and the whole community could work together as a team.

Now, I try to guard my tongue so that I don't hurt others' feelings as mine were once hurt. I cannot control others' actions, but I can control my own. I've also learned that if you can't solve things on your own, someone who cares about you will always be there to back you up. I may not have enjoyed the encounters with Craig at the time, but I became stronger as an individual.

by Susanna Winder, 16
Highland High School
Pocatello, ID

Three Years

When I was in middle school I was bullied. I went to a school called Solomon Schechter Day School. At this school they have very small classes of mostly twelve and sixteen kids. These same kids have been together since kindergarten. I came to this new school from Glastonbury public schools. I was in for a big surprise.

They never called me because I always had to call them. They thought that living in Glastonbury was far away, but it wasn't. Since they thought it was so far away they rarely came to my house. Even when I thought I had friends, I really didn't. They were only "pretending" to be my friends. You have to be really cruel to do that to someone. I went home and practically cried because these people are so mean. I stayed there for the Jewish education that I needed. When we played outside I played with these kids, but I knew deep down that they didn't want to play with me. It made me feel sad and lonely. My whole self esteem went down and I wasn't happy. I always had a smile on my face just so no one knew how I really felt. One day I couldn't take it anymore! I had to tell someone besides my family.

There was this one particular girl who was my "friend". I

told her about how I felt. She didn't believe that it was true. She just replied by telling me that everyone is friends with everyone. My family and I knew that statement wasn't true.

Those three years were the worst! Just talking about it makes me quiver. Those sixteen kids thought they were all that and a bag of chips, but to pick on someone else means that your are not. If they have to pick on me to feel better, that's wrong. If I could go back I would have stood up for myself and said "Hey, what is wrong with me? I'm cool." Maybe not exactly like that but similar to that. I think that if I had done that they would have stopped bullying me.

I always thought that bullying meant pushing someone into a locker. That's mainly what the message is on TV or in the movies. Its definitely not like that at all. Just by calling someone a bad name or even telling them that their hair is wrong is all different kinds of bullying. You might not even know when someone is bullying you because it doesn't seem like it, but it might be. All I can say about those years is now I have learned that being mean to someone else isn't cool. Now I have great friends and friends I can trust. I know that for a fact that they wouldn't bully me because they love me for who I am. Those kids from Solomon Schechter Day School didn't care about me or love me for who I am. Bullying is wrong and if you can stop it good if you can't then ask someone to help you because too many people need your help.

By Tiffany Renert, 15
Glastonbury High School
Glastonbury, CT

A Person of Dignity and Worth

Have you ever been bullied? How did you feel? I know I have been bullied, I felt worthless. I always asked myself what I did that was so wrong. I hated being in people's jokes. My peers would make fun of me because I was over-weight, or I had a bad case of head lice, or even about my back-it looks like a hump. So they called me a camel, a hunch back of Notre Dame, even a whale. I really didn't appreciate them teasing me the way that they did.

Sometimes I would come home and cry in my mom's arms. I always wonder what I did to have them bully me. I really couldn't help it that I had a bad back or I had a bad case of head lice. I asked my mom what I should do, and she said to just ignore them, I thought to myself, "What good is that going to do?" I decided to take her advice, I didn't listen to them. But they still kept the teasing up. I thought, "Why isn't this silent treatment working?"

I still came home hurt. I didn't know what else I could do, nor did my mom. She thought about getting the principal involved, but it would be too embarrassing, so I told her that, that wouldn't be a good idea. I think I will still use the silent treatment, and pretend nothing was going on. Then finally, after weeks of using the silent treatment, they stopped bullying me.

I learned a great lesson, that we are all different in are own ways. Konstance Dambraski once said, "I am a valuable person with dignity and worth, what I do makes a difference." What this quote means to me is that no matter how bad you are made fun of, you are still something in some one's eyes. My mom always had us use this quote; "treat others like you would like to be treated." I have always gone by that quote when I was growing up. I learned a lot by this quote and Konstance Dambeaski's quote.

We are all the same even though we don't look the same as the person next to us. We are all different in our own ways. If kids are making fun of you just remember the quote by Konstance Dambraski, "I am a valuable person with dignity and worth, what I do makes a difference." You are worth something in someone's world. Don't forget that.

By Stacey M. Keller, 16
Highland High School
Pocatello, ID

Chapter: 4

Cyberbullying

How can you protect yourself from online bullies?

The Bullying Blues

I'm sure we all heard of the blues as a type of music, but today in our world children across the nation face "The Bullying Blues." Why does it happen? How can it happen? What type of people would scar other people by bullying!? Those are some of the questions many people ask but they never find the answer.

All human beings have flaws and flaws are what bullies prey on to bring us down. Many kids get victimized and it needs to stop to make the world safer and to stop "The Bullying Blues." For me, being thirteen and in middle school, it is an area were bullies lurk around just waiting for their next victim to hurt, torture and tease.

During the past school year I was instant messaging my friend. We talked about the average things teenagers talk about like T.V. and music. Then I got my friend's message and it said, "Hey, Joe, you know that loser kid that I tease at school? I just e-mailed him and called him a whole bunch of curse words. It was hilarious. I think I made him even cry, knowing him."

I never thought that my friend would do that. I would never pick a bully as one of my friends. I knew that was not nice and I knew I had to put my foot down before it got serious because I know when you're bullied you feel humiliated, defenseless, and afraid.

My next IM was to my so called "friend." I wrote that "it was horrible and disrespectful for you to do that to another human being and if you don't agree with me we could end our friendship."

In about five minutes I got an IM back and it said "Yeah, Yeah, I guess you were right. I was just teasing him. I didn't think it was that bad. Any way I just IM'd him and told him I was sorry." What I learned from this catastrophe was that talking the problem out can fix the problem.

I think the kid that was getting picked on was very sad and who can blame him because anyone who is being called names would be sad. I think my friend felt cool and he thought he was a big tough guy but now that it is all done he knows never to bully again.

Bullying is destroying the life and safety of other people through teasing, bullying, hitting, or otherwise "putting them down." It is as destructive to themselves as to their victims. All those words I said is what I want you to keep in your mind with you when faced with a bully, remember never get down by "The Bullying Blues!"

By Joey Zigarelli, 13
Belleville Middle School
Belleville, NJ

Bullying My Sister

There are many bullies around the world. People get picked on for all the wrong reasons, for how they look, how popular they are and even what race they are! It just so happens my sister Kaity was a victim. This is her story …

Over the summer my family and I went on a vacation to Italy. We had a great time, but something was bothering my sister. She said she didn't want to talk about it. When we arrived at our villa, Kaity went directly to the phone and called her best friend Stephanie. What I overheard was heartbreaking! She said that this girl named Dana was bullying her. She went to the computer and used my sister's screen name to curse and use inappropriate language towards my sister's friends.

When we returned, my sister went to the computer and explained to her friends that she did not say those things. It was Dana's fault. A lot of her friends believed her but it was a different story for some.

I felt terrible! My sister didn't deserve that disrespect from Dana. To make Kaity feel better, my family and I took her to her favorite place to eat. Then we dropped her off at the movies with her best friend Stephanie. When she finally got home, I could see she had a smile on her face once again. That smile soon faded when Kaity went online, and Dana was on. Dana instant messaged my sister and started speaking to her using vulgar language. Kaity was strong and stood up to Dana. She had finally stopped bullying my sister. Kaity had a smile on her face and was happy again!

From this situation between my sister and Dana, I learned a lot. I learned that people bully because they have something going on at home and want attention, or they are jealous of you. Or they are under a lot of stress so they take it out on an innocent child.

I think that bullying is a horrible thing. It needs to be stopped before someone gets physically hurt. I also think that people should try to work things out and help a bully find a new perspective, maybe try to work things out by talking about the situation.

I really hope that something will be done about bullying. Kids that are being bullied should tell an adult or work things out with a person that is hurting them in any type of way. If you're a person that is experiencing bullying problems, try to work things out before they get worse, or tell any responsible adult.

By Kristina Maiello, 12
Smithtown Middle School
Saint James, NY

The Internet Bully

When you think of bullying, you usually think of an older kid calling a younger kid names on the playground, or something like that. It can also happen in other places.

One day, my friend Melonie asked me to come over to her house. Melonie had just turned twelve a few weeks ago, and she had gotten a computer for her birthday. We decided to get online and instant message people. We instant messaged our friend Beth, and to our surprise, she wrote back. We chatted with her for about five minutes when some one with a user name we did not know sent us a message. We sent him back a message. He wrote back, telling us that he knew where we lived, and if we did not give him the answers to the math homework, he would hurt us. Melonie and I were scared, so we did what he asked. Everything was fine until about a week later, when it happened again. This time, though, he wanted us to type his book report for him. Melonie was going to reply when I got an idea. I told Melonie to reply yes, and then print out the message. When she asked why, I told her my idea. She said okay, and print-ed it out. The guy then told us that he would put the book report in Melonie's mailbox. He also said to put the typed book report back in Melonie's mailbox by tomorrow morning, or else. We got the book report and started typing. We changed some things, though. We worded one paragraph exactly like a book report I did last year, then printed two copies. We put a copy in Melonie's mailbox, then I took the other copy and went home.

The next day, I went to Melonie's house before school. We got the message and the book report, then left for school. When we got to school, we went straight to the principal's office and showed him. He was shocked that such a thing would happen. He told us he would ask all the English teachers to read their classes book reports, and find the one we wrote. At the end of the day, the principal came on the intercom and asked for Melonie and I to come to the office. When we got there, we saw a boy named Todd sitting next to him. The principal said it was Todd who had been sending us those messages. Todd apologized and said he only did it because his grades were dropping and he could not play football if he failed. Needless to say, Melonie and I decided not to chat online for quite a while!

Bullying is mean-spirited, cruel, and wrong. We should all work together to stop it. Without bullying, the school and world would be a much better and easier place to live.

By Audrey Lindsey, 13
Forney Middle School
Forney, TX

Get a Life Already

Last year I had an experience with cyber-bullying – while I was at school – and to this day, I still don't know who was doing it. Here's what happened.

I went into my computer class. There were about thirty kids in my class and none of us were really supposed to be on AIM (AOL Instant Messenger), but everyone was on anyway. I was talking to my friends online for a few minutes when I was IM'd from someone whose screen name looked familiar to me. For the sake of this essay, let's call their screen name "JustPlainLoser."

Anyway, it took that person all of about five seconds before they started taunting and teasing me. They teased me about my weight, and they teased me about my religion. Then "JustPlainLoser" went into this thing about how they knew a lot about me and that I obviously had no clue who they were.

The first thing I did after getting the rude IM's was block the sender's screen name from being able to IM me again. However, for some reason they were able to unblock it. This went on for about three days until I just decided to ignore "JustPlainLoser" and let them talk.

I have to admit that their teasing didn't really scare me, but I was a bit angry and confused over the whole situation. It annoyed me enough that I wanted to figure out who it was that was being so rude.

I tried to find out who "JustPlainLoser" was. Eventually I did find out who the screen name belonged to, but that person said that it wasn't her rudely IMing me and that her screen name had been hacked recently. I didn't have any reason to believe her, yet, I left it alone.

I learned some important things from that experience. The first is that there are people out there who are, in my opinion, just plain losers. They get some sort of pleasure for making others uncomfortable online and maybe in the real world as well.

The second thing that struck me was that "JustPlainLoser" was pathetic. I mean, someone has to have guts to say something to your face, but when they have to hide behind a screen name to insult you like that, well, that's just sad.

The third thing that I learned was that "JustPlainLoser" was just like any other bully. If a bully doesn't think they're having any affect on you or scaring you, they just leave you alone. Bullies in my opinion need to see the affect of what they are doing to get their jollies. If you ignore them . . . and that's really easy to do online . . . you're taking away the only reason that they are being a loser in the first place.

So out of this odd experience I did learn some things that have helped me grow. Thank you "JustPlainLoser" for being a just plain loser.

By Rachael Olan, 16
Houston Learning Academy
Sugar Land, TX

The Bully Behind The Keyboard

Megan had always been an honor roll student. She enjoyed studying and was always happy to help her classmates by tutoring them after school and on the weekends. For Megan's 13th birthday, her parents surprised her with a brand new computer! She was so excited. She was thinking of ways to help others. She decided to set up her own web site to help classmates with homework and class projects.

At school the very next day, Megan passed out cards to everyone with her web address. She told her classmates to check out the site and she would be more than happy to help them. The first few weeks went great. Megan kept her web site updated and she posted homework assignments daily in case anyone forgot or was out sick and needed to know what the homework was. She was getting very popular. The teachers were very impressed and were always bragging to the other students about how "smart" Megan was.

One night while Megan was checking her web site, she came across a very nasty posting. It said that Megan was nothing but a teacher's pet and the only reason she had friends was because they were using her to get good grades. At first, Megan just tried to forget.

But soon, the bad postings were on her web site everyday. She would delete them as fast as she could, hoping other students did not see them. She did not know who this person was. It is so easy to hide behind a keyboard.

Soon, all the students who visited Megan's website were talking about the unpleasant postings. Most people took Megan's side and told her to just ignore the postings. She began to feel very uncomfortable in school, knowing someone in school was bullying her from cyberspace. She wanted to continue to help her friends, but did not want these postings to go on. She had never been bullied at school before, and this was just awful. She began suspecting everyone and spent so much time worrying about this, her grades began to fall. For the first time ever, she was not an honor roll student.

Megan's principal called her into the office and asked if there was anything she wanted to talk about. Megan had not told anyone about the postings. She began to cry. She explained to the principal what was going on that she wanted to keep up her website because she felt she was doing a good thing. She had helped so many people. She did not want to let this computer bully win. She said the worst kind of bully is one who does the bullying in secret.

The next day, the principal called a special meeting at lunchtime. He let everyone know that Megan had a new web site address and that every posting would go to his web address before it would be forwarded to Megan. He said the new site was being made so Megan could get extra credit for the help she offered and the school would pay the price for the website. He never mentioned the nasty postings at the meeting, he did not want to upset Megan anymore. This was his way of letting the bully know that he was on to him.

Several days later, the principal called Megan into the

office. This time Megan didn't cry. The principal's way of handling the situation had worked. They never did find out who had been sending Megan the unpleasant messages. The important thing is, they stopped. Now Megan was able to help her classmates without being bullied.

By Taylor Michelle Syslo, 12
Bridgeport Middle School
Bridgeport, WV

Noob Way to Insult Someone

I think that one of the most annoying things that happens online now is a form or cyber-bullying which I'll explain. I like to play RPG's (role playing games). Of course there are lots of players online playing the games. Some are newer to the game (I play two or three different ones) and some have played the game for a long time.

In this one game I play there are different rooms and each room has an owner. They're like the founder of that room and can decide things like who gets to stay and who has to go. Anyway, I was playing this one game that I had been playing for a while. I wasn't an expert yet, but I did play the game for several weeks before this incident occurred.

What happened was that the owner of the room called me a "noob" when I didn't know exactly how to do this one thing. Calling someone a "noob" is like being called stupid. The word is used to describe someone who doesn't really know what they are doing. This other player not only called me a "noob" but also told me that he and nobody else in the room wanted me around anymore. That was weird, because we had had so much fun every time I played the game before. We joked around and stuff and I never got the feeling that anyone in the room was not liked.

When the other player called me a "noob" I found it very rude. It made me angry, because I really did know what I was doing. There was just this one thing that I wasn't sure about. I told the room owner that I was mad and then he said he was going to kick me out of the room. That made me even more upset, because I really like that particular online game.

One of the things I've learned from my parents is that if someone tries to push you around or challenge you, it's okay to push back, especially if I can do it in a way that helps the other person understand my point of view. So I told the room owner that he or she had earlier told me that they were there to teach others players and to help me learn how to play the game. So I asked the room owner why he or she was now trying to insult me by calling me a "noob" and why they wanted to kick me out of the room.

To my surprise the room owner apologized to me and told me that I could stay in the room. I don't know exactly what they were thinking, but maybe they were just in a bad mood. Anyway, I'm glad that I made the effort to stay in the game, because as I said I really enjoy playing it. It taught me that I don't have to just take what someone else says and that I can win by standing up for myself.

By Michael Olan, 12
The Honor Roll School
Sugar Land, TX

The E-bully

Have you ever been bullied? Not very fun, is it? This story is about a smart kid who turned into a bully.

Jonathan was a good kid, but he didn't pick his friends very well. His friends weren't the meanest people in the school, but they were close. Jonathan never dreamed of being a bully. Before becoming a bully, he had tried to help the kids in his class who were not doing so well in that particular class. But now, after watching his friends a little while, he had decided that bullying looked kind of fun.

His friends told him that since he had the Internet, it would be easier to make fun of people and not get caught if he did it on the Internet. Jonathan decided that the Internet was the way to go. Since he didn't need help with homework, he decided he would ask for money. Nobody knew his username. He emailed a girl named Lindsey and told her to leave $5 in her mailbox for him to collect tomorrow, and if she did not do as he asked, or told anyone, he would spread a rumor about her. Lindsey did as Jonathan asked. Jonathan thought this was an easy way to get money. He did it again, and this time he told Lindsey to leave $10 in her mailbox tomorrow. She did as he asked.

Her mom asked her why she needed so much more money now than she ever had before. Lindsey told her mom the whole story and her mom said that she would tell the principal at her school to see if he had an idea on how to stop this kid before they went broke. They talked to the principal, and they came up with an idea.

Lindsey's mom installed a miniature camera on her mailbox and they caught Jonathan. He had to give all of the money back, and had in-school suspension for one week.

If you know someone like Jonathan or his friends, tell someone. Ignore their threats. Don't feel as if you can handle it alone. Everyone needs help sometimes.

By Tori Danae Turner, 11
Winder-Barrow Middle School
Winder, GA

Chapter: 5

The Golden Rule

List some ways can you and your friends can use the Golden Rule to help stop bullying:

Bullies vs The Golden Rule

When I think of a bully, I think of someone who doesn't follow the Golden Rule. Bullies usually boss people around and make them do things that they do not want to do. They don't care that they are hurting people's feelings and embarrassing them. They judge people by what they look like on the outside instead of what they look like on the inside.

A little boy named Andrew was being bullied at school. Three kids were blocking him from using the bathroom! When Andrew got home from school every day, he would run into his bathroom. After three days of this, his mother finally asked him why he does this. Andrew started to cry! He told his mother what was happening at school. The next day, Andrew's mother called the school to talk to the principal about the problem. The three boys were called into the principal's office. They were warned and told this better not happen again, or they will be expelled from school.

Two days later, Andrew's mother asked him if everything was going okay at school. Andrew told her that the same boys were now calling him bad names and blocking him from using the bathroom! Obviously the bullies did not take the principal very seriously. Once again, Andrew's mother called the school. The principal called the three bullies into his office the next morning. He made them apologize to Andrew and they were expelled from school and could not attend any extra-curricular activities associated with the school! Andrew was much happier now that he was not being bullied!

Unfortunately, there are bullies in every school. The students need to stick together and help their friends when they see someone being bullied. Each of us should learn how to stand up for ourselves and not be afraid of this kind of person.

Bullies are people who are not happy about themselves, so they try to make other people unhappy too. They really just want attention. If you are a bully, you need to remember to treat others the way you want to be treated. You will end up with many friends and you will feel much better about yourself.

In conclusion, remember, there will always be consequences for your actions because you may not realize it, but there is always someone watching you.

By Logan Riley, 12
Valley View Middle School
Germantown, OH

Too Close for Comfort

Do unto others as you would have them do unto you. This is what we tell ourselves, instructing one another in this "Golden Rule." But we don't apply this rule to ourselves. Peoples' lack of compassion for one another manifests itself in the home and at school, particularly the latter. My younger brother has become a victim of bullying.

As a twelve-year-old boy in middle school, my brother is far from popular. Luke isn't like most of the other kids at school. What's worse is that Luke knows it. My brother has mental and physical disabilities including slight autism and ADHD, so he is a participant in the special education program at his school, which immediately sets him up as a target. Though we don't want to admit it, we think differently or less of a person who is different or has a disability.

As Luke goes through his day, lessons about science and history aren't the only things he hears. The rumble of conversation in the cafeteria isn't the only sound that reaches his ears. As he walks through the halls, enters a class, his ears pick out what people say about him, their laughter. "You see him? He's dumb," "He's such a klutz," "He acts like he's five," are everyday noises in his world. Although they may seem like harmless remarks to some, the effect these words has on Luke isn't so trivial. The constant barrage of offenses that scratch him penetrate his mind. He thinks less of himself because of what people say.

Unfortunately, words aren't the only weapon people use against him. Until recently, Luke had been able to avoid getting hurt physically. On the way to his science class, he walked through a downstairs hallway where no teachers were. His aide, who is supposed to walk with him to and from classes, was back in his previous class discussing a matter with the teacher. An older boy was walking with his friends in front of Luke. When Luke walked by, the boy pushed him against the wall and scraped his arm. The other boys laughed as my brother hurried away, once again he was a victim of bullying. Because there was no adult in the hallway, the attack went without punishment – the boy walked away without guilt, without consequences.

How would this have been different if bullying didn't happen? How much better would the world be if people had compassion? How different would it be if we practiced what we preached, if we used the Golden Rule instead of throwing it aside? Talking about bullying isn't enough to change it. We need to start the change with ourselves in order to change others.

By Natalie Dumsha, 16
Northeast High School
Pasadena, MD

Try It, You Might Like It

Treating others the way you would like to be treated (A.K.A. "The Golden Rule") should be taught to children before they ever start school. Parents can do this by treating their children how they believe their children should treat others. When small children treat others disrespectfully, parents need to discipline their children in a loving way. Lessons about bullying have to start at home.

Bullying can start at any age. It can be as simple as calling your brother or sister "dumb." The person being bullied ends up with hurt feelings and lower self-esteem. When kids get to school bullying becomes a bigger problem.

Teachers have to listen to students who tell them about bullies and believe them. Kids who are accused of being a bully need to be watched closely by teachers. A lot of the time teachers ignore kids who tell on other kids and label them as "tattle tails." This just makes a victim feel worse because it's not important enough for the teacher to do something about it.

To stop bullies everyone has to get involved. That means kids or adults who witness bullying cannot remain silent. Kids who see other kids bully someone have to be brave and stand up and tell the bully what they're doing is wrong, but also let an adult know.

The Golden Rule is a lesson we all need to learn in our homes and schools. Bullies, victims, and witnesses can be taught this lesson through role-playing, books, videos, and everyday experience in the home and at school.

Bullies need to be treated well by their teachers and classmates. The reasons they became a bully needs to be talked about so that they can learn new ways to deal with their problems. Showing a bully kindness is one way to help them learn the Golden Rule.

Victims need to be taught why bullies bully others, that it's not their fault they're being bullied. The Golden Rule can be shown to them by teachers and classmates showing that they care about them.

Witnesses to bullying need to be taught how to speak up and help the victim. They could be the one to teach both the victim and bully the Golden Rule. If enough witnesses would do this, there would be less or no bullies at all.

I plan to try it at my school. I hope that others will try it too. Try it, you might like it – The Golden Rule!!

By Erika Loesch, 13
Washington Middle School
Washington, MO

Are You A Bully?

When I think about the word bully I think of someone that feels bad about themselves so they have to pick on people to make themselves feel better. Some people can bully by starting rumors or actually pushing another person around. Sometimes bullying can take place in groups to intimidate you. Sometimes a person might become a bully because of their home life. Maybe they get pushed around by their parents or called names. They might feel like they don't belong or have siblings that have made fun of them.

I know a boy who got picked on for little things such as the clothes he wore and his personal features. During school he would get his books knocked out of his hands. He would get pushed into lockers and called names. This boy played football so he knew he couldn't fight back. He ignored the bully, but he still gets bullied today because he didn't do anything about it.

These are some of the things the boy could have done:

    1. Try to ignore the bully.

    2. Confront the bully about his feelings.

    3. If it gets bad enough, tell a grown-up.

If you don't want to become a bully, keep reminding yourself of the Golden Rule. The Golden Rule is treating others as you would like to be treated. This will help you in relationships and all throughout your life. Being a good person is treating everyone equally no matter what kind of person they are.

By Katelyn Koble, 13
Valley View Middle School
Germantown, OH

My Transition to High School

At the beginning of the first semester I foreshadowed myself doing terrible at high school. In the summer, I went to band camp and found myself following the bass drums, being absent a drum. So far school wasn't looking pleasant.

I awoke the first morning of school at six o'clock, having missed the bus; therefore my mom was forced to drive me. I arrived, barely on time, at the instantaneously boring class of Mr. Hall's. I awoke in a puddle of drool and the beeping of the dismissal bell.

The first days are always the same. Teachers present their rules and regulations. I miraculously surpassed all my morning periods and was on my way to lunch when I saw a terrifying bully confronting a pretty cool kid, I recognized him from my first class. I decided to break it up. I strolled over and said coolly, "Hey, what's your deal ... man." The bully boy turned and replied in his monstrous voice," He owes me money; it's not of your concern, so just beat it dweebo." The kid was looking petrified, sweating profusely as we argued. I told him," If you just leave him be, I'll leave." He stared at me as if taking a mental note and finally managed to speak, "Alright already, gosh!"

I expected something else but he just surrendered the captive and walked away muttering curses under his breath. I made small talk with the kid and afterward we sat down and ate lunch together. I had a good rest of the day and returned home. The next day I came to school proud of my accomplishments and ready for a great new year. I later found out that the bully had been expelled and have had no problems since.

So, right now things are going excellent. I'm in the band as second bass and I'm friends with the kid I helped.

By Devin T. Fields, 15
Capital High School
Charleston, WV

I Was The Only One Not Laughing

Bullying is hurting or teasing others to try to overpower them. I have heard that every seven minutes a child is bullied on a playground, and eighty-five percent of the time no one does anything to help. This morning I saw Spike, the school bully, and his friends gang up on Jordan. They were pushing him around and calling him names. I watched, but I didn't make fun of him. I didn't tell the teachers about it either. I was a bystander and sometimes I wonder what it would be like to be the victim or the bully.

I didn't tell anyone because I didn't want to be Spike's next victim. I watched as they taunted Jordan, and how the other kids laughed. I didn't want to be made fun of. I knew that if I told a teacher about this morning, Spike would hunt me down. I know that teachers say that they will never say your name when they are confronting the bully, but it's like Spike has eyes in the back of his head.

I was a bystander. I should have told a teacher what I saw, but I was scared. I wanted to tell a teacher, but I didn't. I promised myself that if I see Spike taunting Jordan or anyone else tomorrow, I will anonymously report it to a teacher. I tell myself that, but will I?

This morning I saw Spike making fun of my best friend. I reported the incident to one of my teachers. Later today I saw the vice principal come and get Spike out of class. He glanced in my direction as he left. I was scared, but I knew that I did the right thing. I knew in the end that everything would be alright.

By Taylor Nicole Turner, 14
Winder-Barrow High School
Winder, GA

Try To Stop Bullying

Many people are faced with bullies each and every day of their lives. Probably because the people that bully them don't like the way they dress or the way they look. So the person bullying them feels the need to make fun of them, put them down, make them feel inferior to them, and to make them feel weak for their own pleasure. The bully probably doesn't feel very secure about themselves ... Lots of people bully every day. Just calling someone a name is bullying. We all need to try to stop bullying.

There is this girl that I went to junior high with, and her name is "Ashley." Ashley was one of my friends, and she would always get bullied because she couldn't hold still in class, and she dressed "differently." So in class these people would make fun of her, call her names, and tell her to get a better clothes style. What these bullies didn't know was that Ashley's family was poor and couldn't afford all the newest trends or fashions, so she was stuck with all of her clothes. They also didn't know that she had a disease that would make her move around. One day in class these bullies were harassing Ashley and calling her names, I was getting sick of it and told them about her family, and her disease, and to leave her alone. Later that day they went to her house and apologized to her and her parents. They later became good friends.

In my experience with Ashley, I learned that you need to fully understand a person and their lives before you start harassing them and putting them down. If you try to truly understand everyone you meet, I bet that there would a lot less bullying. Because if you truly understand a person you don't want to make fun of them, you want to be their friend and you want them to be your friend.

This is a great example of tolerating other people, and understanding the situation better than you did before. We can be an example to other people by not bullying others. Treat others as you would want to be treated. When I walk down the halls at my school, I hear people laughing at other people all the time and making fun of them. There is this girl in one of my classes, and she makes fun of the other students in that class, because they aren't like her, or they look "different." This girl is not being respectful to her peers. I think this is rude, I also think she needs to be nicer towards others and more respectful.

All in all we all need to be understanding of others and try to be their friend. Just like in my story, we need to try to be other people's friends, and not bully them. We need to try to stop bullying.

By Brooklyn Dawn Smith, 15
Highland High School
Pocatello ID

What action steps can you take to protect yourself from physical or emotional harm from a bully?

About Bullying

Bullying is an inconsiderate, unforgiving matter. Bullying includes; people calling you names, beating, pinching, piercing, pushing or shoving (hurting), stealing your money, taking your friends away, making silent or abusive phone calls, sending you offensive phone texts and posting insulting messages on the Internet or by IM.

I think that the best idea is if a teacher can catch the bullies red-handed, that way, you won't get into trouble from anyone for telling. Don't be tempted to punch back since you may get injured or get into trouble.

On a bus, try to sit near the driver. If you have to walk and you're afraid of being attacked, then change your route. Try to leave home and school soon after or in advance, or ask if you can walk with neighbors who live close to you. If you are going somewhere farther away from your house or school try to go somewhere that probably has CCTV so if you're attacked in the street the police may be able to get proof. There isn't just one kind of bully there are two kinds; one is the bully who beats you up and taunts you, and the kind that is a person who sees it all happen but doesn't do anything about it. People who are being bullied need friends so if you are able to help out somebody who is so miserable, please do so.

You could think about martial arts classes so that you are self-assured and you can look after yourself. If people are making cruel comments regarding you then it may be for the reason that they are jealous. Possibly you're better looking than they are or work harder or maybe the teacher(s) likes you more than them. One technique of handling the comments is just to say "yeah, whatever," every time. The bullies will have worked out what buttons to press to upset you. They may make comments about your weight, your looks, the color of your hair, your family, your schoolwork, if you are popular, if you work hard, if you have a disability, if you are a different religion, color or culture, if you wear glasses, if you have dyslexia, or if you've been out of school because you were sick.

Bullying online means sending emails to different students who have stopped eating because they've been called fat or stupid, or because they aren't as smart as you. There was once a girl who tried to burn her freckles off because of cruel comments. The thing all these people had in common was that they were perfectly ordinary, nice people who had the bad luck to come up against a very horrible person. If you have a cell phone, be careful who you give your number to. If you get intimidating or insulting phone calls or text messages then tell your parents. It is an illegal offense to send offensive or threatening phone messages and if it continues, it can also amount to harassment. The police can, and do, take action for crimes like this.

Body language tells everyone a lot about other people. If you're trying not to be noticed and looking at the ground a lot while dashing into school it can make you more visible. If you look defenseless and weak, you are a bully's target so try to make yourself look tough, but if you try too hard the bully will know you are faking it.

Just don't forget to ask for help. Sometimes bullying can make you feel sad and upset and that being alive isn't worth existing but you will come through it, if you get help as soon as you can.

By Katie Magness, 13
Forney Middle School
Forney, TX

It's More Fun on the Playground

I met Cassie my first day at my new church. My dad had told me that a woman who he worked with had a daughter who was in first grade like me. But when I saw her she was different from everyone else. She was in a wheelchair. I soon learned that she was born with a hip problemt. After many months of being confined to the wheelchair, her doctors finally let her have a walker.

One day we were walking around the playground when a boy named Michael came over. I had heard he was "different," but I had no idea what people meant by that. He started yelling at Cassie. He was upset because the walker was leaving lines where ever she walked. He started kicking her and hitting her, but Cassie was not able to defend herself or run away. She started crying. She didn't know what to do and before she could say anything Michael ran off.

We were in shock. A boy had just beat up someone who could not control what was going on. We were even more surprised because we had never seen or even knew kids could be so mean to one other. We ran to get a teacher, but when we told her, it was as if she didn't believe us. She said she would take care of it, but the teacher took little action.

The next day we asked Cassie if she wanted to stay on the pavement, but she replied, "No, it's more fun on the playground." I had a stronger respect for Cassie after that day. She had already gone through a lot, with two hip operations and years of not being able to walk or run.

But no one could prevent her from her new found freedom; she knew that if she let anyone bother her, then she would never have fun herself.

By Meg Taylor, 14
Glastonbury High School
Glastonbury, CT

Take a Stand

How many people in the world have to deal with bullies in their lives? I am willing to bet big money that every single person has had to deal with some kind of bully. I have had several experiences of bullying, especially with me being the victim or the witness. And even though I am ashamed to say it, I have been the bully a few times.

As I am a small girl, I appear very vulnerable. However, looks can be deceiving. When I was in the third grade, there was a girl who was my age, but much larger than me. She was slower than most people and this, of course, put her at a severe disadvantage. I have long, blonde hair and I often wore it French braided. This girl would pull my hair. It went on for a while with my mom complaining to the principal and teachers, but yet nothing was done because of this girl's disability. After a yank to my hair made me physically sick, I made up my mind to fight back the next time. My only reason for not doing so sooner was that I felt sorry for her. But, luckily, I never had to fight back, for she quit pulling my hair.

In the fifth grade, I got to be a witness of bullying. One day after school, my friend and I were leaving our classroom and there were no teachers in sight. A big boy came up to us and called my friend's mom names. Understandably, she got angry and called him a name back. He got so mad that he started hitting my friend with his math book. I was stunned, so I did not think as quickly as normal, and I just stood there. The whole attack only went on for about ten seconds, but it was enough to leave it imprinted on my memory.

When I was an eighth grader, I had the experience of the bully. It had been a tough day for me and there was a particular boy who was getting on my nerves more than usual. My capacity for containing my anger had grown thin and this was the last straw. I lost it, and started chewing this guy out. I regretted it to the extreme after I had cooled down a few hours later. The next day, I sought this boy out and apologized for my behavior. He forgave me graciously.

Even though I sometimes wish that these things had never happened, I would not take these incidents out of my life. They have given me knowledge that I would not otherwise have. I regret having been the bully, but I have learned not to do it again, and by being the victim and the witness, I have learned how bullying can mess up people's lives.

Bullying is wrong. Take a stand and fight against it. Lives everywhere will be bettered because of it.

By Kelly Wilde, 15
Highland High School
Pocatello, ID

Peanuts

When I was in fifth grade there was a boy on my bus named Billy. People were always making fun of him and throwing stuff at him during class. For some reason the teachers just let it happen and pretended that it wasn't actually going on.

One day we were sitting at lunch and the nurse rushed into the cafeteria. Billy wasn't moving. Then the ambulance showed up and took Billy to the hospital. While all this was going on there was a table of boys laughing hysterically. Later on that day some of the boys got called down the office. No one knew what was going on.

At the end of the day my teacher told us what had happened. Some boys found out that Billy was allergic to peanuts and they put them in his sandwich. Billy had to be rushed to the hospital because his allergic reaction closed his throat up and he couldn't breathe. I felt horrible for Billy. Even though I never took the time to get to know Billy I made him a card and brought it to the hospital. I have to admit there were times when I did join in with the other kids and make fun of Billy. Since the peanut incident I never ever made mean comments to Billy ever again.

Billy ended up switching schools. I felt really bad knowing that my school was so mean to him that he ended up switching schools. If I had known how hurt Billy was actually feeling I probably would have taken the time to get to know him better. I have learned to treat everyone nicely, even if they are a little bit unique or different, because you never know how horrible you can make someone feel.

By Kylee Knights, 15
Glastonbury High School
Glastonbury, CT

Striking Back

I understand how Daryl Gray felt. Gray was a 13-year-old straight-A student when he struck back at another student who had terrorized him for two years. But it was Gray, not the bully who teachers said had tormented Gray and others for months, who paid the price. Gray was sentenced in May 2004 by a Georgia juvenile court judge to 90 days probation and had to pay $332 in restitution to his victim. The bully received no punishment. I, too, am a straight-A student who never gets into trouble. When I was in 6th grade I was physically injured by a student who was bullying me. I was afraid to tell anyone that I had been hurt. Finally, I showed the injury to my mom, a teacher at our middle school. The school resource officer took pictures of my injury and a statement from me. The student received 2 ½ days of in-school suspension. The school could not justify more time out of the classroom because the student was in special education. My parents thought about pressing charges, but one of the student's teachers begged my mother to give the child another chance because he did not really understand what he was doing.

The student continued teasing and tormenting me and others for almost a year. Many times I felt like striking back. Students, and even teachers, told me I should just hit him to show him I wasn't going to take the abuse any more. My parents were worried about me and sought help from counselors. They knew it was not in my character to fight back physically. So I just took the abuse. The counselors told me to understand that the bully was using teasing and aggression to make me feel inferior, but that I should not feel inferior. Again I just took it and went home and cried.

The bullying continued throughout sixth grade and into 7th grade. Finally, after several episodes of sexual harassment toward others, the student was removed from our school. Maybe if I had stood my ground against him others would not have been hurt. My fear of breaking the rules was greater than my fear of him.

Many times the teachers don't see or hear what happens until the victim strikes back because the bullies are so good at flying under the radar. The school officials in Gray's case say bullying is not tolerated. I believe that is the case, in theory, but because most adults – administrators, teachers, and parents – are at a loss for how to stop it, the bullying continues. Until it goes too far.

By Will Kearney, 13
Flat Rock Middle School
Tyrone, GA

A History of Bullying

Bullying is something that occurs every day all over the world. It affects everyone's life whether they like it or not. The old excuse of "it's not my problem" has no foundation when it comes to bullying. The best examples of this are the wars caused by the corrupted governments of communism, and military dictatorships. War affects everyone in the world. Most wars are a result of a corrupt government bullying it's own nation or another nation for personal gain. Let me show you what I mean.

Today we are fighting a "War on Terrorism," a war that started with the Twin Towers being destroyed by two hijacked planes being flown into them. Along with the destruction of the towers came the deaths of thousands of people. The plane's hijackers were traced back to a terrorist group led by Osama Bin Laden. While trying to find Bin Laden we found connections from Osama to Saddam Hussein. Saddam Hussein had gained control of a military dictatorship in Iraq. He then unjustly used it to bully around his own people to do whatever he wanted, even kill themselves in suicide bombings. This bullying has affected the whole world as the world tries to end the terrorism that

these men have created. In an effort to end this unjust bullying we are sending hundreds of men and women into bat-
tle in the Middle East and many have been killed. All of the
deaths and all of the fighting are a direct result of bullying.

From 1939 to 1945 we endured WWII. This war came
about as Adolf Hitler gained control of the German government. He then used his power to wage an unjust war on
Europe. As the war went on, the Japanese, who were allied
with Hitler, bombed Pearl Harbor. This bombing forced us
to defend ourselves by going to war against Hitler and his
allies. We sent thousands and thousands of men into
Europe to stop Hitler and the war. We eventually succeeded, but not before losing tens of thousands of men and
dropping two nuclear bombs on Japan. Although the
United States of America was perfectly justified in going to
war, we are still feeling the affects of WWII, a war that
resulted from bullying.

Within our own nation we have severe cases of bullying.
In our big cities we have gang fights, and drive-by shootings. These fights and shootings occur when the gangs feel
that someone has trespassed on their perceived territory.
Gangs do not own the territory they defend so they are not
justified when they go out and start gang wars to defend it.
This bullying not only kills the members of the gangs, but
also innocent people caught in the crossfire. Now families
and friends are devastated because they have lost a loved
one to bullying.

As you can see, there is no foundation for the excuse "it's
not my problem." Bullying is everyone's problem because
war is everyone's problem. No matter where you go you
will be affected by war, and war is always a result of bullying. It is either one nation or group bullying other nations
as in WWII and the attack on the Twin Towers or in Iraq.

Gang wars have the same elements, just on a smaller scale.

One person or one act cannot stop bullying. We all need to step out from behind the old excuse of "it's not my problem" and take a stand to stop bullying when we see it. We all need to realize that it is everyone's problem and it will take everyone to stop it.

By Jeffrey Carter, 17
Highland High School
Pocatello, ID

A Bullying Experience

When I was in second grade, I was very quiet and mostly kept to myself. I wasn't the most popular, I was simply independent and only spoke to the people I trusted. At recess, I would normally walk around with two or three people instead of actively participating in a soccer or basketball game. My friends would complain daily that they wished they could join in with everyone else, but I was simply content with being on my own and talking with my friends instead of being out on the field. A group of about three girls from the grade above me had the same recess time as my second grade class. I didn't know their names and I had never bothered or interfered with them, but for some reason they chose to bully me. Everyday they would push or shove me and call me names if I fell.

At first it didn't bother me, but when it continued for most of the year it began to affect the way I felt at school and at home. I didn't tell anyone about it for awhile, instead I just went along with it and considered it a part of my day. I know that if this happened to me now I would say something to them the minute they touched or bothered me, but when I was younger I was very shy and didn't want to create problems. Seeing that they were older than me, I wasn't confident enough to stand up for myself and my friends felt the same way. After this went on for most of the year I became sick of it and decided to say something to them the next time they decided to push or bully me. When they approached me I simply told them that I didn't want anything to do with them and I hadn't done anything to deserve the treatment I was receiving. To my surprise, they didn't take it the wrong way and respected me from that day forward. It felt great to be able to stand up to someone and fix my problems without causing more harm on both sides. The very next day after I had asked them to leave me alone, they approached me at recess and asked if I want to walk with them and go to the playscape on the top of the hill.

At first I was nervous because it was the first time they had actually been nice to me, but once I started talking to them, they weren't as mean and nasty as I had thought. After my experience, the group of girls never bullied anyone again and I got to be best friends with one of them and would go over to her house almost every week. This experience has taught me that if something is bothering you or someone is doing something to make you feel uncomfortable, simply try to approach them and tell them your side and maybe they will understand. If they don't, then it is important to tell a parent or teacher so that they can take it out of your hands. If you do not stand up to your fears, you never know how good the outcome could be.

By Jackie Pajor, 14
Glastonbury High School
Glastonbury, CT

Bullies: Mean or Just Self-Conscious?

Bullying is a dangerous activity that can take place anywhere at any time. Bullies often bully other people because they are insecure and take it out on other people. Bullies should be stopped because they affect almost anyone they talk to. Most common bullies are in school. They pick on other people because of their race, how intelligent they are, what they wear or look like, and their disabilities.

Emotional bullying is even worse than physical bullying. Emotional bullying is started by calling another person bad names or by picking on them, if they're different from everybody else. Emotional bullying can cause the person being bullied to be stressed and to have low self-esteem. That can also lead to the person being bullied to commit violence to themselves or others. Emotional bullying usually then leads to physical bullying.

Physical bullying is dangerous and harmful to both people involved in the situation. The person being bullied is not only endangered of being hurt and could even possibly be killed. The person doing the bullying can be in danger of being expelled or sent to prisons for younger people. Physical bullying still takes place in schools, even when teachers are around and it needs to be stopped.

Bullying is bad because it causes the person being bullied pain. Whether physical or emotional that person almost always is hurt by the bully's comments or physical fights towards them. It can also cause embarrassment if kids are bullied in school in front of other kids especially of the opposite gender.

Bullying in schools has to be stopped. Bullying in schools is probably the most common place for it to occur. Some teachers just stand by and watch the kids bully each other, even if they know that it's not an equal fight. They also give both kids detention and expulsion from school, even if one of the kids, just the bully started the fight.

To stop the problem of bullying in schools, assemblies can be shown to provide students with solutions that will help them stand up to bullies. If that doesn't work children being bullied can go talk to a family member or trusted teacher about his/her problem. My last solution to this problem would be to make programs or clubs in the school that support kids being bullied and approach their problem with their bully individually. These kinds of clubs will give children being bullied the feeling of that they're not alone. These suggestions will help make schools safer for children, inside and out.

By Holly Golia, 14
Franklin Middle School
Nutley, NJ

The Boy In The Front Seat

About a year ago, I took a bus to school every day. There was one boy who would enter on at the last stop and quietly take his seat at the front of the bus. The older boys in the back of the bus would constantly bully him. It started when they threw papers at him on the first day of school, gradually this advanced to bottle caps and then they began to attack him verbally. The boy was constantly called, "the bus driver's boyfriend, and the mute." After three months of this the boy slowly took the bus less and less and finally stopped riding it. Throughout the whole episode the bus driver did nothing. Since the kids who were bothering the boy were the oldest kids, no one dared to stand up to them. This situation made me feel upset, because of how hopeless the boy was and the power the older boys were allowed.

I was also really surprised that the bus driver did nothing since she was the only one who had the power to stop the bullying. I was also disappointed in the rest of the kids riding the bus, that they did not stand up and support the kid in the front seat. From this situation I learned to stand up for others. I am sure that the bus ride wrecked the boy's whole school year and ruined his enjoyment of school and making friends. From now on he will carry the scar of the mean treatment of the older boys, and he will no longer have any confidence in himself. I also think that the reason the older boys bullied was because they were bored, and were looking for something to entertain themselves.

I think that this situation could have been avoided if the bus driver or another kid on the bus told the authorities and action was taken against the older boys.

By Liza Navarro, 14
Glastonbury High School
Glastonbury, CT

The Lonely Boy

Last year, during my eighth grade homeroom every day, there was a boy who was made fun of. He was a small Indian boy with a hearing aid. He tried to do his work quietly in the corner but the other kids wouldn't allow it. The group of kids made a contest about who could hit him and how many times they could hit them. Each time something hit him, I saw a painful look in his eye. All he would do is pick the trash they threw at him and he would keep it so he could throw it out later on.

I was surprised that he didn't tell anyone and that he suffered through it every day. He would tell them to be quiet and leave him alone but they insisted on hurting his feelings. They picked on him because he was different. He celebrated different holidays and he had a different skin color.

During this time my friends and I sat there, I felt bad for him but I didn't want to do anything because I didn't want to be targeted. The teacher was always too busy, oblivious to all the activities around her. I couldn't believe that kids could be so cruel to their own peers.

One day, I could see him getting extremely mad and when the next paper airplane hit him, he totally lost it. He yelled at the kids to leave him alone and that he didn't deserve this treatment. He sat down ashamed of himself and of his outburst especially when the teacher, annoyed at the outburst, told him to be quiet and sit down. I saw him burying his head in his hands, wishing he had friends in the class and wishing he wasn't there. This was my first encounter with a major bullying event. I realized that people can be really harsh and unfair. Now that I think back upon the homeroom bullying sessions, I wish that I had stood up for him and made the others stop. I am also disappointed with all the other kids in the class for doing those terrible things but also for not stopping the ones who did do the things.

Also, I went to elementary school with him where he was continuously picked on day after day. Our class, as a whole used to have circle time, where we could talk about our concerns and worries. He brought up his problems and we brainstormed ideas to help him. Although we all agreed to abide by the rules no one actually did. I tried being nice to him and in the halls he would say hi to me. I secretly wished that I could help him and be his friend or get him friends. I can't even imagine the pain and suffering he went through. I wish I had the knowledge of bullying that I have now, back then so I would try to help him.

By Jessica Prior, 14
Glastonbury High School
Glastonbury, CT

Chapter: 7

Stand Up

What ways have you learned that could help you stand up for yourself or someone being bullied?

Woodchuck

The school bus is a perfect environment for bullies to carry out unprovoked attacks on innocent kids. The bus driver is occupied with the road because it is his job to get the kids home safe. The so-called "Silent Witness" cameras are rarely on and can be easily blocked. The camera fails to see what actually goes on between kids who ride the bus. There were many times that I witnessed incidents between kids in the back of the bus, but one stands out in my mind.

I was in elementary school, but in the later years, so I wasn't susceptible to bullying from older kids. The boys in my grade were fooling around in the back seats, throwing around backpacks, telling dirty jokes – the regular behavior. We stopped in front of a sort of dilapidated house with garbage and metal scraps strewn around the yard. A dog that was chained to the garage barked and snarled as the bus pulled up to the driveway. Two kids came out the front door, their frizzy-haired, bath robed mother waving good-bye. The older girl took a seat near the front, but her younger brother ventured back into the middle. He was getting dangerously close to "older kid" territory. He quietly sat down and stared out the window, probably wishing he was anywhere else in the world but on this school bus. Even looking at him I felt pity. He was on the chubby side, obviously not very athletically inclined. He wore a worn plaid shirt, partially unbuttoned to reveal a dirty, white undershirt. A pair of glasses sat on his button nose and chubby cheeks. The boys in my grade looked at each other with glee. He was, of course, ideal prey for them. They all looked to Evan, a perfectly manicured Abercrombie boy, hockey star and all-around great guy supposedly. He grinned and leaned over his seat.

"Hey! Hey, you!" he said, directing his voice towards the back of the kid's seat. "Woodchuck!"

The boys exploded in laughter. They stuck their teeth out and made little animal motions with their hands. I, sitting in the seat diagonal to the boy, could see his face getting red. Jerks, I thought to myself.

"Hey, Woodchuck," Evan started again, gaining confidence with this popular new nickname. "Hey! I'm talking to you, kid. Turn around!"

The boys stopped laughing now. This kid had some nerve, ignoring Evan like this. Evan stole up to the seat across from the kid's and started throwing insults at him. "Hey, was that your mother, Woodchuck? I can see where you get your good looks. I love that fat, sloppy, dirty look you have. Maybe you can give me some fashion tips sometime."

I felt a growing anger in my chest. I felt like a fire was slowly being kindled in my very heart, I was so angry. But I didn't act. I looked pleadingly towards his sister, who was sinking lower into her seat, and the bus driver, who was staring in his side-view mirror. I looked out the window and saw, to my relief, the brick school in the distance. I guess Evan saw it too, because he said, "Until tomorrow then, Woodchuck." He walked past my seat and I glared at him with all the hatred I could muster. But he didn't notice. He was too busy giving high fives and exchanging laughs.

Why didn't I do something? Why do people who witness these acts look the other way? It's hard to stand up for something right when you're going up against the majority power. I still regret today when I turned my eyes away from people in need. But from all the bullying I have witnessed, I have learned that people need my help and I have to give it to them when I am capable.

By Cassandra Pastorelle, 14
Glastonbury High School
Glastonbury, CT

Bullying, The Big, Bad Problem

We all know how it goes, big guy vs. little guy. This is an example of the biggest problem in school, bullying. It goes on in every school and seems that it cannot be stopped. People are afraid to stand up against bullying. Especially when the problem happens to be 6'6" and 200 lbs.

Not much can be done when an adult is not around, but you can still stand up for yourself. Standing up for yourself can make an impact on the bully. He may think, "Hey, he isn't afraid of me anymore" and that could be the end of that. You never know what can happen.

When most people see someone being a bully, they usually just try to act like they didn't see it or that it isn't happening. Imagine if, instead of ignoring it, you walked up to the bully and told him to leave them alone. Bullies don't like it when people stand up to them. It's as if they are questioning their authority. They feel a little weaker.

Think of how more enjoyable school would be without the fear of being bullied. Students would have a better time learning. Stopping bullying would cut the injuries at school to a record low.

Bullying is a problem that has to be stopped before it overruns our schools. Speaking to all the bullies, you don't need to take out your aggression on other people. A school without bullies is a place where I want to be. If we all stand up to the bullies we encounter, we will emerge victorious.

By Robert Emfield, 15
Highland High School
Pocatello, ID

Bullies - All Schools Have Them

Every school has its own widely-known bullies. My school was no different.

It all started in the summer of the fourth grade. There was a girl named Martha who nobody seemed to care for. Not only was she a year older than everyone else, she was also a whole lot meaner than any other kid in the school. She always picked on the kids who seemed helpless. No one ever had the courage to stand up to her, for she was two heads taller than the average fourth grader.

There was a poor, scrawny kid with big glasses and buck-teeth named Norbert. Nobody dared stand up for him. Whoever did was taunted and made fun of for "liking" him. I should know; I tried to stand up for him in the third grade and nobody let me forget it until the fourth grade.

One day at the local pool, Norbert was standing on the low diving board ready to jump in. Nobody had bothered him today, and it seemed like he might even be having fun for once in his life. Then, it started. Martha climbed up the high diving board right next to Norbert. He didn't have his glasses on then, and I don't think that he noticed who exactly was standing next to him.

"Norbert is a beaver! Norbert is a beaver! Go ahead, Norbie, go build your dam, you buck-toothed beaver!" Martha shouted across the diving boards. "What? Who's there? Why are you making fun of me?" Norbert cried, while squinting as hard as he could to see who was there.

"Nobody special, Norbert! Hah! Norbert has buckteeth! Norbert's a beaver!" Her chanting led a group of her friends to start joining in. I felt bad for Norbert, but I couldn't forget the teasing I had put up with for all too long. I wondered whether I should help.

"You leave him alone!" I shouted, not knowing what I had just done. Had I actually stood up for the geek with four eyes? I couldn't believe myself ... did I forget about all the teasing and people making fun of me for that traumatic year of my life? When Martha looked over at me, I could tell I was in trouble. "Oooh! Laura's in love with Norbert! Laura and Norbert sitting in a tree ... k-i-s-s-i-n-g! First comes love ... " It didn't stop for a long time. The song is apparently longer than I thought it was.

"I'm not in love with him; I just think it's unfair that he has to go through this misery while you're standing there putting him through it!" I shouted, sounding much braver than I actually felt. What was I thinking? This girl could take me out in a second! Well, it was too late for Norbert, and apparently a little late now for me to back down also.

"What was that? Did I hear someone standing up to me? Someone who's a whole year younger and a whole two heads shorter than me? Do you really think it wise to be doing this?" Martha shouted, making my stomach jump up to my throat.

Norbert got down from the diving board, ran and got his glasses, and ran back to the pool to see who was making fun of him and who was actually sticking up for him for once.

"Are you ... sticking up for me?" Norbert asked, a look of shock in his face. "Yes, I am. I don't love you, but I do think that you shouldn't have to go through this misery and get tormented all the time just because you're a geek." At this, Martha walked away, apparently very angry that some-one actually stood up for Norbert.

One thing I can say about this situation is that I could tell Norbert was feeling braver, as he had never had anyone that stood up for him. As for me, I was shocked at what I had done, and I felt quite brave about my actions.

Today, Norbert isn't so much of a geek and we have become friends. All because of that one incident, Martha stopped picking on Norbert, and everyone left me alone about loving Norbert.

As for this school's bully, she has not been so mean to people in a while.

By Laura McFee, 15
Glastonbury High School
Glastonbury, CT

The Bullies That Became My Friends

I have had my fair share of bullies. When I was in the seventh grade I was picked on a lot. I was called so many rude names, and it really began to hurt my feelings and my self-esteem. The kids at my school were never nice to anyone except the other mean people that were in their groups.

As time went on the bullies seemed to pick on more people, not just myself. I became friends with a lot more people, and I guess you can say that I was in the more "popular" group. Some of the girls that I hung out with got picked on a lot. This made me upset, and I decided to do something about it. I went to the counselor and asked if there was anything that I could do to stop all of this. She told me that there was nothing that I could do that wouldn't get me into trouble. I slowly walked out of her office, and it hit me! I could treat them with a lot of respect and maybe, just maybe, they would have the heart to change.

The next day I told my friends about it and they thought that I was crazy! Why would I want to be nice to someone who was totally mean to me?! So my friend just walked away when the mean people started in on them. I just sat there, and listened and then asked them if they wanted to come with me to find my friends. They laughed at me and called me a loser. I felt like a loser too, but I thought that if I kept trying to get them to change that they actually would do it! At lunch, the bullies walked by us, looked at us, laughed, and walked along.

About a week later I was at my locker when someone walked up behind me and said "Hey Katie." I turned around to find one of the bullies standing there with a piece of paper. I looked at her, smiled, and took the paper. I opened it, and it said in BIG bold letters "I'm really sorry for everything. You and everyone you hang out with are so nice, and we are so mean to you guys. Can you forgive me?!" I was in shock by now! My plan actually worked. I showed my friends the letter and they all decided to invite her to lunch. She explained why they bully everyone. She said it was because they felt like they weren't as good as us.

This gave all of us another outlook on why people act the way that they do. From that day on the "bullies" sat with us, and became really close friends of ours. They didn't pick on anyone else, instead they became the victims of bullies, and they finally saw what it does to peoples' self-esteem. I'm still friends with all of those girls today, and I feel that somehow I helped influence them in a better way. I showed them that bullying isn't the right thing, and that life can actually be fun in a positive way if that's how you make it!

By Katelyn Frost, 16
Highland High School
Pocatello, ID

Bullying — It's Not Just About Kids

Bullies are everywhere. They are in the halls, on the streets, and always knocking kids down, taking lunch money, or name calling. You see it everyday but there is really no stopping it. People might say that if they saw bullying taking place around them they would do something to stop it but it is really one of the hardest things in the world to stand up to a bully and tell them to step down.

I remember when I was in 7th grade there were always the really cool, popular, "don't mess with me, I'm perfect." They never really did anything to me because I guess I was cool to them. Then one day they began spreading rumers about a really close friend of mine. I knew that they were almost impossible to stop, so I didn't do anything.

All I did was keep telling my friend not to worry and that things will be over soon. Then one day three of these girls walked up to my friend at lunch and started making fun of what she was wearing and how her hair looked. It was awful. Then one of them pulled out an open carton of yogurt and threw it all over my friend. People were amazed. No one had ever seen bullying that badly before and all my friend could do was run away crying.

I wasn't going to sit and watch, I knew I needed to do something. So I got up and walked over to these three girls and told them that what they did was really mean and that they may be so popular that they can get away with things like that. They looked at me and told me that they can do whatever they want and I just made a huge mistake by saying that to them. But I didn't care. I stood up for what I thought and that made me happy.

I was always worried that these girls would wind up doing something to me that was even worse than what they did to my friend but they never did. Everyone was proud of me for standing up and my friend was so grateful. I really think that on that day bullying took a major fall and people were definitely not as mean to others anymore.

But even though bullying slowed down in my school it did just kept going outside of school. My father was born with cerebral palsy, which affects the way he walks or the way he can handle things like scissors or carrying things. He walked with a pretty bad limp all his life.

I will always remember one day when I was about seven years old I was at a restaurant with my parents. I was sitting with my dad on a picnic table when he got up to go help my mom get the food. As he was walking back with the food I heard the lady at the table next to us say, "Look at that freak, he must be a retard or something." Now I was seven years old so I really didn't understand what they meant when they said that, so I asked my dad. He told me about his disease and I felt awful for even telling him what the lady said but he tried to convince me that it doesn't bother him since he had to live with people acting that way.

I knew it still bothered him. And me, being the "in your face" seven-year-old that I was, I got up and walked over to that ladies table and said, "I don't understand why you are saying bad things about my dad. You must be an awful person if you can talk poorly about anyone that's different than you." She just stared at me and didn't say anything. Then I walked away. I was proud of myself. As we were leaving the lady said goodbye and apologized to my father.

From my two bullying experiences I found out that bullying takes place among kids and adults. I know bullying is a really bad thing and I wish something could be done about it. But I've been going to schools where teachers spend a lot of time making things like bullying skits, or doing things to teach people how to handle bullying, but even when teachers see bullying happening in their classrooms they don't do anything. I just think its strange that a group of people can do some much to pretend like they care but when they see it, they do nothing at all.

But now when I see it I make sure to do whatever I can to make them stop. I never want anyone to have to feel as bad as my friend did, or as bad as my dad did. Or even as bad as I did having to witness it, and being confused as to what to do.

By Holly Tamburro, 14
Glastonbury High School
Glastonbury, CT

The Impossible is Possible

Every single day, they called me names. They harrassed me, and thought of nasty things to say as they passed me in the hallways. As the bullying continued, my self-esteem dropped tremendously. It killed me inside. Not because they made fun of the way I dressed, and the things I enjoyed doing, they also made fun of the color of my skin. All the students watched me while those girls tortured me; they would all sneak peaks daily and sometimes even laugh here and there. Everyone noticed, but no one wanted to help me. Someone to stand up for me, that was the one thing I needed more then anything those days. Someone to tell me everything was going to be all right.

I was torn apart, not only physically but also mentally. Anger and frustration filled up inside of me daily, but there was nothing I could do. During that moment in my life it seemed as if this would never change. I used to wish I could just let go someday, be free of all the torture I had to face. I wanted to be carefree again, I wanted friends, but more importantly I wanted to be respected for who I was. I wanted to quit my journey of life. I wanted it all to end. Something inside my heart told me that the impossible was possible. There were those days when I felt so hurt inside; all I could do was cry myself to sleep. I knew that with true dedication I would become a stronger person and I could stop all of this.

With my determination and dedication I did as much as I could. I continued to attend school, but I had a more positive attitude. I was proud of that person I was, and nothing could take that pride away from me. When I saw the girls staring and pointing at me I'd just smile and walk on by. Students started to respect me for sticking up for myself. Occasionally people would come up to me and talk to me about how much they looked up to me. They say I've been a great role model for them. What's even better is that the girls who bullied me finally realized what they did was wrong. They decided they had better things to do with their lives than put their anger on other souls. They came up to me very guilty one day and they finally said sorry to me for all they put me through.

By sticking up for myself, I made so many new friends. I taught others to stick up for themselves. I set a good example for my peers, but most importantly I changed as a person. With hope and a positive outlook on life anything is possible. I learned that even though you may have to fight by yourself at first to achieve your dreams in the end there will be others that will stick by your side. Even though this situation was so hard to deal with in the beginning, I am so proud to have gotten over it. Thanks to those bullies and all my peers I finally realized that the impossible is possible.

By Swara Kantaria, 15

Proclaiming Faith

I have only had one personal encounter with bullying, in which I was a witness. It all took place in my eighth grade history class. My friend Mike* was showing off because the teacher had left the room. He always acted like he was better than anyone else, so it didn't surprise anyone, when he began making fun of one of the girls in my class. Her name was Rachel*. Rachel was very quiet. Her family did not have a lot of money, and lived beside the town dump. At the beginning of the year, I had tried to befriend her, but she closed herself off. Rachel was very religious. She always carried a Bible around with her and wore a cross around her neck. On her binder she had placed a sticker that said, "Spread God's Word." We all accepted her for who she was, but when Mike decided to make fun of someone, no one was immune. Mike flashed Rachel a smile, and sidled over to her desk. She looked up shyly, unsure what to expect from this guy who had never before acknowledged her. Mike grabbed Rachel's Bible and began reading. I cannot remember which passage he read, but it had to do with not having sexual relations before marriage. Rachel's face went from pink, to a deep crimson. Mike continued to read until someone threw a pencil at him to make him shut up. Angered by the gesture, Mike put the Bible down and began to speak to the class. He talked about how stupid it was to follow a religion. None of us could believe our ears. Then he grabbed Rachel's binder and tore off the sticker. We were shocked. Rachel sat, huddled in her chair, crying silently. Her religion was being trash-talked to her face. Filled with rage, I stood and faced Mike. "What is wrong with you? Why can't you leave her alone, can't you see she's upset? It used to be funny, but you took it too far," I said, loud enough for the whole class to hear. Mike, shocked, opened and closed his mouth as if he was struggling for air.

Later that day Rachel came up to me in the hallway, and thanked me. She told me how humiliated she'd felt, and how ashamed she was that she could not have taken a stand herself. I told her that she had been upset, and it wasn't her fault. Mike was the only one to blame for what had happened. We sat down at a lunch table and began talking. We have been good friends ever since.

When I think back, I think that Mike was probably feeling insecure, which led him to make fun of Rachel. It made him feel powerful, and in control. Rachel, of course, felt sad, alone, humiliated, and violated. From this experience, I learned that the only reason people bully, is to make themselves feel important. I also learned that by stepping in, one single person can completely change the situation.

By Elyse Pizzo, 15
Glastonbury High School
Glastonbury, CT

An Angel At My Side

Ever since the reign of man, as far as I know, there have been people who feel they are inferior to others. Some people even push others around to establish this inferiority. These people are commonly known as bullies. I cannot think of any personal acts of bullying, but a bully tried to push me around after school when I was in kindergarten. Then one day a silent kid, who I had never heard speak in my life, helped me solve my problem.

After school each day my brother and I would walk to my aunt's house. We would wait there until my mom picked us up after work. There was one quiet kid who would walk behind us a ways, and another kid who would walk the same direction on the other side of the street. Every day was the exact same thing. We all walked the same direction and in the same way. Nothing ever went wrong for a long time, and I'm not sure what sparked the kid, but then one day he snapped.

In the process of walking home one day, the kid across the street said something very rude to me for no particular reason. I don't recall ever even making eye contact with the kid until that day. I had never even heard him speak until then. As a result of my efforts of drowning him out, he became even angrier. He started to yell things at me that I had never heard a kid say before. I don't recall what he had said to me that day, but I do remember how I was feeling as he continued to taunt me. I remember him crossing the street toward me, and my brother telling me to walk faster. I also remember being scared. I thought, what could I have done to provoke this behavior. I felt helpless myself and my last option was to run. I thought about just taking off, but he was older than me and I knew he would catch me in no time. Then all at once it seemed like an angel stepped near to my side.

Although my savior was human, he bailed me out none the less. The older boy who had followed me home day after day was standing between me and the bully. The bully was surprised at first, then he scowled and walked toward him. The boy met him half way and told him to walk away. The bully didn't say anything but he did back away. The older boy looked back at me and told me to go home. As I walked, I could hear the older boy talking loudly and questioning the bully about his actions. At that moment I felt a great love for the boy who went out of his way for me. After that the bully never said another word to me.

As a result of someone elses kindness, I was comforted with a feeling of safety. Being bullied is an awful feeling, and I feel badly for any person who endures it. My hope is that they never give up and they go out and make a name for themselves. I personally think bullies are looking for satisfaction for themselves and pushing others around is how they get it.

In my case somebody stood up for me, but who will stand

up for every other defenseless child out in the world. It has to start with each individual person standing up for what they believe is right. More likely than not, someone will stand with you. You never know, but you might even save some kid's life.

By Tyson Taylor, 16
Highland High School
Pocatello, ID

The Hardest Obstacle of All

On a playground, kids usually fall, scrape a knee, or hurt themselves, but did you know every seven minutes a child gets bullied? However, the sad part is 85% of the time no one does anything to help. Did you ever have to come to school in fear of getting hurt on a daily basis? Well, 30% of the U.S. students in grades 6th through 10th have reported moderate to frequent involvement in bullying, either as the bully, victim, or both. Something needs to be done to keep U.S. private and public schools safe and free of violence. Bullying needs to be stopped, because it is becoming a hobby for kids in everyday life.

Bullying is not a cool thing. Kids that get bullied are more prone to become a bully, or have a hard life. When kids bully, it really hurts the victim more than it seems. Some kids can take teasing, but usually it pecks at a kid's heart until they feel as if they can't go on anymore. This is one reason why every 18 minutes in the U.S., a kid dies from suicide. Some people wonder why kids bring guns to school, and why they shoot anyone in the way. The truth is these kids take their anger out in their peers. These kids are really hurting inside. When they shoot, they really don't care who they kill. They just want revenge. They want someone to feel like they did when they were bullied. Therefore, they result to violence. I believe if something were done about bullying, the rate of violence in schools would decrease. What could we do? How can we stop these cruel kids from ruining innocent kid's lives?

Nearly every school has a teacher "on duty" when kids are at recess or lunch. This is a helpful solution to stop bullying. However, I have noticed that some teachers "on duty" don't pay attention. They are doing other work or grading papers, and frequently don't look up. Sometimes, things happen, and the teachers don't see them because they're looking down. I have noticed only two problems with this solution, the one I have just stated above, and the situation of not having enough teachers "on duty". The teachers have a lot of area to watch. It is nearly impossible to keep your eyes wide open if you have to watch all around you. Schools need to increase the number of teachers "on duty." This would make it a lot easier on the teachers, and it would make our schools a safer place.

Sometimes, all a bully really wants is a friend, but he does-not know how to make one. In a bully's mind, all he's doing is "making friends." So, sometimes becoming a bully's friend may make the bully stop his cruelty immediately. I believe the only way schools can stop bullying is by increasing the amount of teachers "on duty" in the hallway, cafeteria, gym, and outside, or they can try to help by talking about bully prevention on a daily basis. All of these things can help, and can keep all of our schools safe.

Bullies shouldn't have to be a thing to be scared of, and kids shouldn't have to live their lives in fear. Sometimes, life brings obstacles in many sizes, but bullying shouldn't have to be one of those obstacles you can't face. To stop bullying in public and private schools will not be an easy task, but in the long run it will be worth it. If you ever get a chance to confront a bully, or help a bully's victim, do it. Don't just stand there. Remember, one can make a huge difference, doesn't 1+1=2?

By Rachelle Melancon, 14
Buras Middle School
Buras, LA

Is It Worth Losing?

Egregious. Daunting. Ghastly. It was the day she saw her for the last time. She was definitely involved, and she knew it. "Could this day get any worse?" she thought to herself. First, her friend was furious with her. Then, her friend moved away. She let her tears of agony and anguish flow right out of her. That girl was me.

Although I was only in third grade at the time, that day still comes to me with special clarity, as I pondered it in my mind and heart. My friend, Emma, had been bullied since the first day of school. I knew about it, right from the beginning, but never took action. Although there was this little peevish voice in my head that kept reiterating, "Do the right thing. Tell somebody," I couldn't. It wasn't that I didn't want to; I just wasn't allowed to. I wasn't permitted to free Emma from all her misery. "You tell one soul, and you're dead meat," the bully said. It was a threat, and I had accepted it. Kids could be so cruel. I knew my friend was hurt, physically and mentally.

Emma urged me to tell somebody, but I was too terrified to do anything. "Please tell someone. I beg of you. If I tell, the bully's will deride me even more. You're different. You can tell someone!" Emma would plead with me everyday, but I chose to ignore her request. I was afraid that if I got involved, my life would become just as bad as Emma's, maybe even worse.

Time flew by quickly, and my life was spiraling downhill. It was the middle of the school year, and nobody knew what I was going through, nobody. I felt as if I were keeping a secret, which if revealed could dramatically change my life. Everyday, Emma would have to face the bully. I figured that if I kept to myself everything, I knew, my life wouldn't be as dreadful as Emma's. But, I had it just as bad.

I could see in her face that Emma had just about had it. I thought she was angry with the bully, but it turned out that she was mad at me. "You know, I thought you were my friend. I thought you would help me out. I bet if that bully drove me to my grave, you wouldn't care." she blurted into my face one day after school.

I stared at her dumfounded. "You know I can't tell anyone." She nodded her head slowly as she said, "Well, it doesn't matter anymore. I'm moving!" I couldn't believe it. I started crying helplessly at the thought of my only friend, leaving me once and for all. I had never felt so desolate in my life.

The next day, I went to get Emma so we could walk to school together, but she was gone. Her house was empty! She didn't say goodbye or anything. She had left me there, without a goodbye. There was a note pinned to her door that read, "To: Ann." I didn't have the courage to read it at that time, so I put it in my backpack.

In school, we were discussing our work for math, the subject that usually thrilled me. But I just couldn't concentrate. I had to read Emma's note.

"I hope you know how much I hurt
And what I had to go through.
I wished that you would tell
But I guess it was over you.
I really considered you a good friend
But when you broke my heart
That was the end!"

The poem gave me the strength to do what I should have done earlier. I told Mrs. Tokees about the bully after class. The bully was then suspended and transferred to a new school. If only I had the courage to do that before. Now that I look back at this incident, I wonder, was Emma really worth losing? I could have saved Emma from all her pain and misery. I had the option of either saving Emma or keeping silent, and I had obviously chosen the wrong one.

If you are ever in this situation, and have the choice of keeping quiet or standing up to free someone from their pain and sorrow, do the right thing. Remember, you have the option; you just have to make the right choice. It might just be enough to save a friend and stop a bully!

By Ann John, 12
Belleville Middle School
Belleville, NJ

Why Are Some Kids Bullies?

Bullying is a very mean and sometimes hurtful action. In my opinion, it is right under no circumstances. The bully usually feels cool, tough, or even powerful when they bully. The kids who are bullied usually feel very embarrassed and often feel the need to seek revenge. I also think that when you witness someone being bullied and do not do anything to stop it, it is just as bad as bullying itself.

Often, while a bully is being mean to someone, it makes him or her feel better about him or herself. Sometimes, they get a sense that they are cool, tough and even funny. Also, when others begin to laugh or just pay attention to the bully, it often makes the bully feel even more popular, and can sometimes lead to him or her picking on other kids more often.

Bullying is right under no circumstances. When a group of kids is bullying someone, and another person decides to join in to try to get noticed, it does no good for anyone. Bullying is really just an inconsiderate action, and should be taken very seriously.

When someone is bullied, he or she usually feels humiliated and embarrassed. Also, many times people can feel self-conscious about how they look, and even angry. A friend of mine, who sometimes gets bullied often feels rage towards the bullies. He wants to stand up for himself, but gets worried that he will be made fun of even more. These are also common feelings for kids who get bullied.

Sometimes, when you watch someone being bullied, it is just as bad as bullying. To just stand there and watch a fellow student get made fun of is something I cannot do. I feel I should stand up to the bully and let him or her know how it feels to get bullied. I feel it is just not right to make fun of someone, especially when the person getting bullied has not done anything.

In conclusion, bullying is wrong, no matter what the situation. When someone is being bullied, fellow students should stand up to the bully. If all bullies would stop making fun of kids, the world would be a much happier place.

By Laura Urbanovich, 13
Franklin Middle School
Nutley, NJ

Afraid

Many people can describe bullying in different ways: teasing, calling people names, hitting other people, and even ignoring them. The only way I can sum up bullying is feeling afraid. My friend was not afraid of the 'in' crowd though, even though they would bully him daily. He never wanted to do anything about it. I never quite understood why until the day they came after me, too. I felt put down and alone. I would believe everything they said about me no matter how farfetched it was. Then, I read something from one of my books. It read; "No one can make you feel inferior without your consent." Eleanor Roosevelt had said those words. I finally understood them and I was going to do something about the bullying.

The next day, I stood up for myself and my friend. They never messed with us again, or at least not in front of me. I knew I had made a difference to an extent but I also knew that there was still bullying going on in my school. I felt bad knowing I could not stop it from happening. People were spreading rumors and harassing people because of their skin color, social status, and friends. Sometimes, the bullies did not even really know the person they bullied. I know I cannot stop bullying completely. It is in every town in every country. I do think I can make a difference at my school though, and I feel it is the best I can do.

I think that bullies are also afraid. They may be afraid that they will not be cool if they do not pick on someone or that they do not want to be the victim first. When one of my other friends would invite my sister and me over to her house, she would talk about my sister behind her back.

Even though she had claimed to be her friend, she wanted to be cool with me because I was the older one. She was afraid I would not like her if she liked my sister. I would not be surprised if she ever talked about me behind my back though, too. She tried to hang out with us both, but when my sister left the room, the ugly words came rolling out. Bullies may even have problems at home or feel upset but they still do not have a good enough excuse to make people feel unwanted. I pray every night for those bullies because they have their own problems to figure out. I hope that someday, we can stop the bullying. The world would be a better place to live in and the people would be less afraid.

By Taylor Rexrode, 13
Forney Middle School
Forney, TX

Chapter: 8
Take Action

Who do you think could take more action to help stop bullying?

Bullies, Bullies Everywhere and Not a Friend In Sight

"I can't understand why people are frightened by new ideas. I'm frightened of old ones." - *John Cage*

This quote explains why many bullies bully – other kids' differences. I have been a victim before, so I know how it feels. I believe that one of the reasons might be that the bullies need attention.

I was born in Michigan. I had lived there for most of my life, and I was fairly happy. I had a good school, good friends, and nice teachers, too. I've always been top of my class. I was a grand prize winner in a writing contest. After that, everyone in the school respected me. I had made my school look really good.

Then my dad got a job here, in California. After a long discussion, we decided to make the move. I was in second grade then, and I was very excited at first … but only at first. Shortly after the move, I began to discover that this California school wasn't like my Michigan school at all. Even though it was a private school, no one there acted that way. The teachers paid no close attention to bully situations at all! The education there made me look like a genius, and that made other kids in my class feel inferior.

I felt hurt, sad, lonely, and I even wished I wasn't smart! I tried to tell several teachers, but they didn't do anything. After almost a whole year of being bullied, I realized that these kids were only teasing me because I was smart. They were jealous. That thought gave me self-confidence, and I started to stick up for myself. When the year was over, my family and I decided that an independent study program would be better for me. Now I have made a lot of friends at my dance class. I am much happier away from bullies.

I want to be a teacher when I grow up. I think I'll help stop bullying if I do. I would introduce the idea of a special teacher, or counselor, that helps children become who they truly are inside. The counselor would have the kid take a little survey called "all about me." The questions would be about the kid and what happens at home and at the school itself. If the counselor figures out something that could be the reason the kid is bullying, the counselor should then contact the kid's parents and classroom educator. That way no one will feel discouraged about learning like I did. Instead, they could be encouraged to learn! After all, Albert Einstein did say, "If at first the idea is not absurd, then there is no hope for it."

By Maria Grekowicz, 12
Mother of Divine Grace School
Ojai, CA

Bullying — There Are Solutions

Bullying is a major problem in our communities and schools. It is also the most common type of violence in our society today. Basically thirty percent of the students are bullies or victims to this harassment. Bullying is even against the law. During bullying there is always a bully and a victim. There are also solutions to this problem.

First we have the bully. A bully is someone who directs verbal or physical aggression toward someone else. When they do this they are trying to gain power over the person they are directing this harassment to. Most likely they are trying to get attention because they feel unnoticed. When people see bullying going on and they direct their attention to it by thinking it is funny they are really just encouraging the bully to keep at the harassment to the individual they are doing it to. Then they will try to find new victims to add to his bullying.

Next we have the victim. The victim is someone who continuously is exposed to aggression from peers in the form of the physical and verbal harassment. The victims are usually the ones who are weaker than their peers. They also have very few friends if any at all and are not good with their physical appearance. The victims also usually get left out of school activities. When they are left out like this it can make them very sad and emotional and not want to be seen in public.

Last there are ways to fix the bullying problems or there are solutions to them. The main way to keep bullying away from our society is to keep a positive school environment. A way to do this is to make rules that can be easily understood. You can also try to keep the classes small as possible because research says less violence is reported out of smaller classes. Another way to stop bullying is to get parents to teach children the appropriate skills at younger ages to keep them from being a bully.

Finally I've reached my conclusion. I've told you all about how bullying is a major problem in our communities and schools today. I've also told you about the bully and the victim. Then I told some of the solutions to the bullying problem in our society. Maybe after you read this you will know how much of a problem bullying is today. Maybe it might even make a difference somewhere in a community.

By Mathew Webber,
Homeschooled
Mount Tabor, NJ

Are They Really Your Friends?

By lunch on the first day of high school, I still hadn't made any friends. I walked into the cafeteria and saw a group of girls sitting at the table next to the door. One of them called me over. She introduced herself as Meg. "You're new right?" she said. "Yeah …" I replied to the question with uncertainty. "Well, you can sit here with us if you want." Wow, maybe I had finally made some friends.

I sat at the table and listened to the girls' conversations. They didn't stop gossiping about other people. Then I heard them talk about a girl named Jackie. "Wait," I asked, "isn't Jackie your friend?" "Yeah, but did you hear about her dad?!" "No, what happened." "Well, he had an affair, and he was living a secret life with other children and everything." I didn't know what to say, why would they talk about their friend like that? Lunch was over, and I only had one more class left until the end of the day. "What class do you have next?" asked Laura (a girl from the table I was sitting at) "Oh, I have English." "AWESOME! Me too! Walk with me!" she told me. We walked into the English room and Laura ran over to a girl and hugged her. Laura introduced her as Jackie. "Oh, hi Jackie," I said. "Hey! You're the new girl right? What's your name again?" "I'm Grace" "Cool, wanna sit with me and Laura?" English wasn't bad that day; it just hurt me to see Jackie being so oblivious to what was happening. Meg and her friends were all making fun of her, and Laura (who was friends with Jackie) just let it happen. Later that day, I found out that Jackie was also on my bus, and she lived down the street from me.

A couple of months later …

Jackie and I had become good friends and the incessant gossiping about Jackie and her father hadn't stopped yet. I wanted to say something, but I was so afraid that I would become the loner again. "How does everyone know about my dad?" Jackie asked. She was sitting on the floor of the locker room crying. "Why won't people leave it alone? It's not any of their business! Who would say this about me?" "Uh … Jackie … um … " "Spit it out Grace" "Uh … well, I know who spread the rumors?" "WHO?!" "Well … it was Meg and her whole 'gang'." "No way, they wouldn't do that to me…I'm their friend …" She looked at me with big eyes, and I just wanted to cry. It was so hard for me to tell her that the people who she thought were her friends, were the ones who were making her unhappy. "No, they're not your friends. They talk about you every day at lunch and I've wanted to say something for the longest time, but I just couldn't tell you, they wouldn't have talked to me again!"

PHEW! It was off my chest and it felt so good to just let that go. "Grace, I can't believe you didn't tell me about this before!" Jackie sounded betrayed. "Jackie, I didn't know how you would react." "Fine, well you can just listen to them talk about me … I thought you were a nice person, guess I was wrong." On my way home, I noticed what looked like some dark paint on the side of Jackie's house. Confused, I walked by to get a better look at it. I was speechless! It looks like someone had thrown toilet paper all over her house. Profanities were painted on the sidewalk around her house. She's such a sweet girl, who would ever do this to her?

The next day, I walked into the lunchroom and walked right past Meg's table, and I sat by myself. Meg came over to where I was sitting (followed by her posse) and said "Did you see it?!" she asked. "See what?" I was confused, but then she continued by saying, "HER HOUSE!!! IT'S GREAT ISNT IT?!" I should've said something, but I didn't, I just sat there absolutely astonished...How could something like this happen to a nice girl like Jackie?

By Grace McConville, 14
Glastonbury High School
Glastonbury, CT

The Three Things I Will Do

After Ms. Staggs' presentation on bullying, I began thinking about what I can do to help our school become bully- and collusion-free. The fact that I am in SAVE Club is beside the point; it struck me as terrifying that in our school our behavior and words could change someone's life. One small thing can make a HUGE difference. And if one small thing can make a difference, imagine three things! I decided to do my best in these three things: be friendly to my peers, tell an adult when bullying occurs, and be more of an individual.

Being friendly to my peers is my first step in helping. If I am nice to everyone at school, then no one will be offended by me, which means that my chances of being bullied are slim. To decrease anyone else's chances of being bullied, I will not exclude anyone, that way they can't be picked on by anyone else. I will also refrain from back talking in order avoid bringing kids' self-esteem down.

Another thing I will do to help make our school bully-free, is inform an adult when bullying occurs or if I have knowledge that bullying is going to occur. Telling an adult is not the same as tattling. Tattling is to get someone in trouble, telling, on the other hand, is to get someone out of trouble. I know that the adults that I should tell at school are teachers, the SAFE coordinator, guidance counselor or any staff member that I know can help. Telling a trusted adult can help prevent someone from getting hurt, and prevent any further bullying or collusion.

Becoming more of an individual is one thing I can do to help prevent collusion in our school. Collusion is when someone sees something being done that they know is wrong and they go along with it. To be an individual person, I can dress the way I feel no matter what everyone else is wearing. That also means that I won't have to hang out with the "popular group." I can be with people who like me for me! Individuality is what makes this world interesting and diverse.

I'm very committed to making Windy Ridge a collusion- and bully-free school. I'll start by being friendly to others, notifying an adult when bullying is occurring, and thinking more for myself. I know that I am unique from my peers and I will show that it's good to be different. Windy Ridge will become a collusion-free and bully-free school and I will do all that I can to make that happen!

By Carmen Adriana Clemente, 12
Windy Ridge School
Winter Garden, FL

How Bullies and Victims Become Friends

Hi. My name is Matthew. I have never really experienced bullying myself. I am basing this story from what others I know who have experienced bullying told me.

One day my best friend named Martin was carrying his books to math class when he stumbled and dropped his books. Paul, who was feared by everyone in sixth grade, started laughing. Now Martin was embarrassed.

When they got to math class, Paul told everyone Martin was clumsy. Then everyone laughed. Because everyone laughed at him, Martin cried. Since Martin cried, Paul called him a sissy and the class laughed harder. Then the teacher came in and settled the class down.

After math class, Martin went to the principal's office and told the principal that Paul was making fun of him. The principal said that she would keep a close eye on Paul. She asked Martin to tell her if Paul did it again. She said that bullying would not be allowed in school and Paul would get in trouble. Because the principal said she would keep an eye on Paul, Martin felt a little better, but still he was angry.

When Martin got home from school that day, he told his parents what had happened. His parents told him that everyone drops their books sometimes and that he should not let Paul's comments get to him. They said that crying did not make him a sissy and that he had been brave to stand up for his rights by going to the principal's office.

The next day the guidance counselor went to each class and told everyone the consequences of bullying. She told them that bullying hurt other people's feelings and would not be allowed in school. If caught, they would be sent to after-school detention and could be suspended if the incident was bad enough. Then she showed the class how bullying hurt other people's feelings by asking for volunteers and pretending to bully them. In math class, she picked Paul and pretended to make fun of him.

Paul realized that laughing at someone else was wrong. Paul apologized to Martin. After that day, Paul never bullied anyone again.

By Matthew Spicer, 12
Bridgeport Middle School
Bridgeport, WV

The Truth Behind Bullying

The fact is bullying is becoming a serious problem in schools across America. However, people don't really understand all of the aspects of bullying and why it occurs.

People generally think of bullies as being large, obnoxious and intimidating. What they don't realize it that it is usually the most insecure kids that bully others. The ones with problems at home, or are for some other reason emotionally unstable, are the ones that feel the need to put others down. Bullying is sometimes a cry for attention.

Bullies think that they look cool or tough because they make fun of others. They feel the need to hurt other people because then they think they'll get respect. Unfortunately, the plan usually backfires. They don't get respect. Instead, everyone becomes afraid of them and tries to avoid them. They aren't able to make many friends and this doesn't help their emotional insecurities.

The bullies I know generally never think about the effects that bullying could have on their victims. Victims who have been bullied could become scarred for life or extremely uncomfortable with themselves due to unpleasant childhood experiences involving bullying. Many psychological problems could stem from past bullying experiences.

However, despite all of these problems involving bully-ing, there is not enough being done to prevent it. There are certainly guidance counselors talking to students about bul-lying, but most kids won't want to listen to them. This country's schools really need a more effective way to deal with bullies.

As a solution to bullying, famous, influential people need to talk to kids about bullying others. Kids are more likely to listen to their role models about things like this. These influential people need to stress the fact that everyone has feelings, and that no one wants to be ridiculed or singled out. Everyone wants to belong and be accepted amongst his or her peers.

Overall, people need to truly understand bullying and why it occurs. They need to understand the mindset of bul-lies and the state of their emotional health. Also, people need to find different approaches to end bullying in American schools. By helping America's children, we will help America's future.

By Emily Hazzard, 14
Franklin Middle School
Nutley, NJ

Bullying - A Weak Man's Form of Strength

I was born and raised for a third of my life in South Africa. In this mainly black dominated country, my family and I were known as minorities. However, my father and mother believed it would be best for our family to move to a safer community for my two brothers and I to grow up in. Coming to America at a young age was very hard, because everyone seemed to have their own group of "friends" and none of which seemed to be very open towards me joining them. Throughout middle school, on a daily basis I was verbally bullied because I was a white African - American and I too had British/South African accent (which "made" my family different from the other kids).

However, I quickly learned to tune all my frustration into the sport of golf. Everyday after school I would come out and play by myself and hit range balls vigorously on the range. However, golf has always (hopefully not in the future) been a male dominated sport, so once again I was bullied as being a minority in the sport. This, however, only made me stronger, because I would only practice harder and become more devoted towards this tedious sport. After a couple of summers and a great deal of practice, I became one of the most prestigious golfers in the Roanoke Valley as well as one of the top in the state. I was offered many full scholarships to colleges all around, however, I chose JMU (no scholarships) because I believe I will come out a better golfer.

As for the guys that had once teased, they offered for me to play golf with them on a regular basis and highly respected me. After I had earned a name for myself, the guys at my school also seemed to develop respect for me and have not bullied me since.

Knowing that there were many situations like my case, I desperately wanted to do something about it. During my junior year in high school I joined Cave Spring High School's South County Coalition (this group's main priorities were to prevent underage drinking and bullying) to hopefully prevent or make some kind of impact on bullying cases like mine. I believe that bullying is man's weakest form of strength!

By Vicki Kasza, 17
Cave Spring High School
Roanoke, VA

Bob's Best Friend Joe

Chapter 1

Have you met Bob? This is Bob. Ok, so maybe you really do not want to know Bob, but he is a protagonist in this story. Bob is in the sixth grade, only he looks like he could wrestle my dad and win. Of course, he is on the football team. He is also on the soccer, basketball, swim and baseball teams. He loves sports so much that I think if he could do it without having everyone laugh at him, he would join the girls' softball and field hockey teams as well. His love of sports might have something to do with his dad being the football coach; then again, it could be that he does not seem to be good at anything else.

How about Joe? Joe is a victim and he is a natural. If you look in the dictionary for the definition of nerd, geek or victim, there is a picture of Joe. Not that he isn't a nice guy. He never stands up for himself. He always wears glasses and dorky clothes. Most kids make fun of him or at least avoid him.

There is not a day that goes by where Bob does not harass and belittle Joe. Every time I see them together, Joe is picking up his books, getting out of a locker or apologizing to someone for "accidentally" being pushed into them. It is more than just the Jock vs. Geek thing. Bob really seems to have it out for Joe. Poor Joe!

I am living proof that being a nerd-geek is not contagious. You see, I am Joe's friend. I am also on the football team with Bob. I cannot agree with the way that Bob treats Joe. I do know that nothing is ever as simple as it looks. There has to be a reason Bob hates Joe. If I could only get Joe and Bob to realize they complement each other, they could be good friends.

Chapter 2

Joe sees Bob's dad yell at him about his grades. He initially feels happy that Bob is in trouble. Joe tells me about it and we hatch a plan. Joe thinks I am insane.

Chapter 3

Joe offers to help Bob with his grades if he is allowed to eat his own lunch. Bob is not interested until he fails a test. Out of desperation, Bob asks for Joe's help. Bob passes his make-up test.

Chapter 4

Bob and Joe become friends. Bob's dad and teachers are happy about his grades. Bob stops giving me grief for having Joe as a friend.

By Jonathan Sinkkanen, 11
Bridgeport Middle School
Bridgeport, WV

The Butt Head

Why is it that people without physical and mental handicaps think that those with these conditions are the perfect target for ridicule and exploitation? There is a cancer survivor in my class, and consequently he is hearing impaired as well as other physical handicaps. From the radiation he has a bald spot on the back of his head. The boys call him "Butt Head" because it looks somewhat like a butt cheek. They also refer to him as a freak.

I have never witnessed this happening to him because I assume these boys know that it would make me mad. But I have heard his mother tell my mom how they have done cruel things to him. It simply broke my heart to hear her relive these awful experiences. I know that as a mom she wants to protect him, but she cannot always be there. She is so thankful that he is alive, and she does her best to ensure that he lives as normally as possible.

Of course my mother wanted the friend's mom to call the parents of the boys who were bullying. I think my mom might have been right. That was when they were much younger, and I think that the parents could have been more positive role models at the time. Many parents would be terribly upset if they knew what their little darlings were doing as soon as they were out of sight. Of course there are those who have the "Out of sight, out of mind" philosophy. Those parents really don't want to know what their child is doing.

The school has a responsibility to protect the students, but the teachers and principals see that only as being from bodily harm. Their solution to verbal attacks usually is to ignore them. That is not a solution, and it will not make it easier for the person being bullied. The younger the child, the more responsibility the teachers and parents have for correcting that incorrect behavior. A child who is allowed to bully becomes an adult who bullies. The younger that children are taught tolerance, acceptance, and anti-bullying skills, the better off they are. Have you ever watched a bunch of pre-schoolers play? There are already those who take away the others toys and are pushy and bossy. A child cannot become a responsible, productive member of society without guidance and nurturing from a caring adult. Can you start teaching them too early? I don't think so.

Do we need to better educate our teachers on how to handle bullying? Posting signs up everywhere that say there is an Anti-Bullying policy is not enough. Teachers need to be more aware of what is going on around them. We must all work together to end bullying in schools, on playgrounds, and in the workplaces.

Anonymous
AR

Take Action

I remember when I was in the fourth grade. There was a girl in my class who wore old, junky, torn, and ugly clothes. She had messy hair and smelled bad. She got picked on a lot. One day, my friends were making fun of her because of those reasons. I was just standing there, feeling sorry for her. I was confused. I didn't know what to do, I couldn't move from where I was standing. I just stared. Then I snapped out of my trance when I remembered something a wise person once told me, "you're just as bad as the bully if you don't take action". I knew she was getting hurt, so I took action and stood up to them. I said, "You guys, just because she's different it doesn't mean you can make fun of her.

The outside of your body doesn't make a difference, the inside does. On the inside, she's just as good as you and me." Then, I invited the victim of the bullying to sit with me at lunch and play with me during recess. She gladly accepted. I was very proud of myself and my friends learned a valuable lesson. They didn't bully her anymore after that. A lot of situations like that happen. I think we should stop bullying now before it gets way out of hand.

My principal tells us excellent speeches about bullying. A lot of people get value from them. They give you courage to stand up against bullying. I think all schools should have sessions about bullying. That would make a difference.

I also think that if more schools had uniforms, kids wouldn't get bullied about what they wear. Schools should have worse punishments and stricter rules against bullying.

We could live in a better school, community, and world if bullying weren't a huge problem like it is now. I'm saying that you can make a difference, so take action!

By Miranda Kafantaris, 11
Walkerton Elementary School
Walkerton, IN

What questions do you have about bullying that you could talk to a trusted adult about?

Not Like This

Picture a crowded school bus. It is early morning, and the sun is just beginning to peek through the wispy clouds. The bus driver is calmly ignoring the muffled calls of "Cut the apex! Cut the apex!" from a brown haired boy in the third row, instead concentrating on the road in front of her. Now put a skinny bespectacled eleven-year-old girl in the seat behind her, holding a book and trying desperately not the punch the flaxen haired guy sitting behind her.

That would be me. See, there, with the glasses and the book? And the reason I'm trying not to punch him is because he is, once again, bullying me. He never leaves me alone; every morning it's taunt after taunt until I want to explode. He has told people loads of rumors that are so untrue it isn't even funny anymore. And the worst thing is, he just won't take a hint, just keeps coming back with more.

"Hey, Freak-o, whatcha reading?" he says, leaning over the seat and snatching my book out of my hands. "The Fellowship of the Ring? You have that many brain cells, Freak-o?"

At that point I snapped. I whipped around, glasses crooked (they always are) and punched him right in the nose. If I hadn't taken karate two years previously it would be funny, but as it is the blonde boy doubles over, dropping my book and clutching his face. And, while I'm sitting there, kind of dazed about what I just did, I start to wonder: Why do bullies do this to people? How can they make me feel so trapped that I act out of pure instinct, not even knowing what I'm doing, like a dog? What is it that makes bullies act like this, preying on younger kids? Is it because they don't have caring parents, or because absolutely no one tries to stop them?

In fact, 85% of students these days report seeing people being bullied and just walking right on by and another 30% report being either the bully or the victim. I think this is completely cowardly. Why can't we just confront these people while we have a chance? Stop bullies before they destroy your life, and, in the end, theirs as well.

So what makes a bully what they are? Well, why don't we explore that enigmatic shadow that is their mind, for starters? Hang on, this could get very gnarly very fast.

Most bullies bully people because of their own problems (an uncaring family, parents that drink, or, in some cases, being bullied themselves). Some bully because they want to be "cool." Some even bully because they saw others doing it first, and wanted to join the gang. Bullies are all ages, so don't expect your little sister to be angelic just because she's five. Even in preschool, children were beating on me, and I can't be the only one. But, no matter what age kindergarten or college, Internet or face to face, bullies are still bullies. Help the world: stop them while we still have the chance. Help them see that what they're doing is wrong.

Witnesses (a.k.a. the scumbags) are easy to figure out. They're simply there to watch you fall, to laugh at your pain. I've lost friends that way, as well as earned black eyes.

But what about the victim? What do they feel? That's easy: you're talking to one. Most of the time I feel trapped, and angry. It's like when you get really mad at someone, and all of a sudden you just want to run, run far and fast, away from them and keep on running until you pass out or die. It's hard to explain this feeling. It is, in essence, the primordial fight-or-flight situation. When somebody starts beating on you, yelling insults in your ear, everything just kind of fades out until it's only you and them and the wide-open spaces to run to. And your mind just goes blank for a moment, with one thought drilled into your brain: I don't want to die like this.

Stop bullies. Help people like me and like all the other even less fortunate out there. Help them see the error of their ways. I don't want to die like this. Do you?

By Delphine Kirk, 11
Thompson Middle School
Murrieta, CA

The Walk By

There was a group of boys at my school who were bullies. A lot of kids were scared of them and avoided those kids as often as possible. Half of the school had become innocent victims of their cruel intentions. And I can tell you that I was not about to be one of them. I felt that if I was to get on their good sides then they wouldn't pick on me like they did the other kids. I figured that if I hung out with them then they would like me.

Well anyways, I was in 7th grade and it was after school. I was hanging outside with these kids pretending to like them. I probably shouldn't have been with these kids but I oddly enough felt like if I was with them they couldn't make fun of me. We were just talking and throwing rocks when my friend from my English class walked by.

His name was Steven and he was kind of a geek. He was the typical nerd who wore high waters and the same worn out grey sweatshirt every day. His hair was long and greasy and he had pretty bad acne. I felt bad for him but I was his friend. Underneath his appearance he was a good guy. He was nice and very genuine. I liked him. When Steven walked by, the kids that I was with started taunting him. They were making cruel comments like "Hey grease ball, go take a shower," or "Go get a new sweatshirt, you look like trash." He looked like he was about to start crying. I wanted to do something but I was scared. I didn't want to step in and have them start saying that stuff to me. The part that hurt me the worst was that look that Steven gave me. Steven finally walked away with his head down low and tears in his eyes. I felt horrible.

The next day in English class I apologized to Steven. I told him that I felt terrible for not stepping in. He forgave me but I still felt like I should have done something. To this day I will never forget that incident. Now whenever I see someone being bullied I step in. Steven made me realize that you have to look past appearance and accept people for who they are. He also taught me that bullying is not ok and it really can hurt people.

Bullying goes on in every school, in every town, in every state, in every country. I could most likely guarantee that there is not one kid in this whole world who has not either been a victim, had been a bully, or witnessed an instance of bullying. They are taking steps to stop bullying but it will unfortunately never stop. There will always be people who think they're better than someone and will pick on people. Bullying is wrong and that's that.

By Lisa Scougall, 14
Glastonbury High School
Glastonbury, CT

Have You Ever Seen Someone Get Bullied and Did You Help?

Have ever seen someone get bullied before and if you did, did you help them? Well here's a story about how I saw someone get bullied and didn't help them. And you would have thought that me not helping one little person would not even matter, but it did.

It all started when I was walking down the hallways of Lilburn Elementary. You see before I moved here I use to go to school there. When all of a sudden I saw some guy slam this kid to a locker, so I hid behind a wall. The kid was Michael, a young 4th grader, and the bully was, Tommi, a new 6th grader. I knew Michael but, Tommi just came to the school. Tommi was telling Michael to give him $1 for an ice cream, Michael refused. So, Tommi punched him in the eye. And Michael started to cry. And then I coughed so that Tommi would mistake me for a teacher and just as I thought, he did. He ran faster than a car. After Tommi left I came over to see what had happened to Michael. I picked him up off the ground and asked him if he was okay. He looked at me and asked,"Why didn't you help me?"

I said, "I ... I'm sorry, I was afraid." And his response tore up my heart. He said,"It doesn't matter if you were scared, but you think about how I felt?" And I just looked at him and left. Of course, he went to the office to get some ice for his eye.

I felt horrible about what had happened and couldn't forgive myself for not helping Michael. After I left him there I went to my bus to go home. While I sat on the bus I saw Michael being picked up by his mom. She looked furious and it made me feel bad for not helping him. I just thought if I had helped him he would be okay and I wouldn't have so much guilt to deal with.

The next day it turned out that Michael got transferred to a new school. I thought it would be a better place for him, where he wouldn't get bullied anymore. I was so very wrong. He got bullied there to, but I felt so guilty I went to solve that problem. I went to Michael's school and talked to the bully. And no, I didn't beat him up. I told him that if he didn't want to get into trouble he would stop. And so he did and now Michael isn't mad at me anymore and I don't have any more guilt.

I learned very valuable lessons that if some one is in trouble, help them. So, if you know someone that needs help, help him or her before they get hurt.

By Hanh Truong, 13
Buras Middle School
Buras, LA

Bullying is An Issue

When I thought about going from sixth to seventh grade, I was pretty nervous. I didn't know what to expect. I was entering a new school. I was going to now be educated at the new middle school, Smith Middle School. I had heard lots of gossip from everyone talking about how it would be totally different from Gideon Wells, my old school. They said that the classes would be larger, the atmosphere would be different, and the people would be meaner.

On the first day of school, we had a large assembly filled with our whole seventh grade. It was amazing to see everyone after the long two months we had for the summer. All of the new cliques were forming and everyone seemed so different. I looked around at all of the people that I was friends with in elementary school and in my classes the year before and everyone seemed so much more distant and mature. After I finished scanning the crowd, the assembly began. We were introduced to all of the principals and guidance counselors and everything was going fine. Next, they started to hand out guidebooks of rules and regulations. The first thing we all noticed was how colorful the guidebooks/planners were. The principals and guidance counselors told us to flip to several different pages about all kinds of topics such as grades, cheating, sexual harassment, etc. Then they told us to flip to the section on bullying. As I was turning the pages to find the topic, I thought to myself about how ridiculous it was to talk about this, but I eventually found the page and just remained quiet in my seat. As they started to talk about it, my friend and I just looked at each other like this was a waste of our time. They kept telling us that if we witnessed someone getting bullied to tell a teacher or try to stop the situation.

Once the assembly ended, my friends and I just went off to lunch. When we entered the lunchroom it was pretty much the same as when it was in sixth grade. You had your popular table of girls and guys, the middle class area, and the nerd tables. I just sat down with my usual friends and lunch was great. The rest of the day was fine and I went from class to class filling out information about myself for all my new teachers. When I got home that day, I told my parents how school was, did some of my homework, watched TV, and went to bed.

The next morning, I got into school a little bit earlier than the day before and not a lot of people were there. To waste some time, I thought I'd walk around a little bit. When I got into a certain area of the school, I saw these big, tough kids that I assumed were eighth graders. They were talking to some short, scrawny kid. Actually they weren't talking, they were yelling at him. They were saying something about how he was such a nerd and that his mommy probably picks out his clothes for him. I was so afraid for this kid. When the kid tried to walk away from these other people, they tripped him and all of his books flew all over the place. Right then, I realized that this kid was getting bullied. Even though the teachers at the assembly had told us to tell a teacher about the situation or try to stop it, I was also afraid and just continued to watch it happen and eventually walk away.

After I got back to my locker, I thought about that poor kid. Why didn't I say something? I could have done something for him. But instead I just ignored the situation. I should have told a teacher or something, but I didn't.

That day I learned that bullying is still a very big problem with our society. When I was first told to look out for bullying at the assembly, I thought it was ridiculous, but now that I know that this is an issue, I try to help out when I can with people that are having problems with other cliques or other people that are just out to get them.

By Courtney Andries, 15
Glastonbury High School
Glastonbury, CT

Cursive Names

Sticks and stones may break my bones but names will never hurt me is an old saying that does not hold true meaning. At our school and probably others, the kids in Math Counts and Chess Club get called geeks, the smart ones who don't put down their teachers are teachers' pets, and the overweight kids are called fat. The kids who love computers are nerds, the ones who love drawing and Yugeo are weird, and the popular kids are the ones who give every group their names. Mainly, they are the bullies.

The popular students say "How can we be bullies if we don't physically hit anyone?" I'd know why they are bullies for I'm a victim, physically and verbally. You can even be bullied in band. That is the worst class for me because a kid who plays drums likes me, but he always hits me with his sticks. I ask him to stop but he says he's joking around, but the bruises on my body tell me it isn't joking around.

I've been treated pretty well considering how other kids in my school have been treated. For example, this new kid calls another kid curse words, geek, and even steals and hides his things. I think that is an awful thing, and most of it happens in the school cafeteria.

The cafeteria is a room where rumors or phrases about unpopular kids start. The room is full of conversations about kids behind their backs. There are rumors about people's best friends, lies from one to another, and now since we are in middle school, break ups from boyfriends and girlfriends. Whenever someone breaks up with someone, they say things behind the other person's back or verbally bully them.

People are so bullied by appearance, even when there is a beautiful person inside. For popular kids, it's the opposite meaning – pretty on the outside and ugly on the inside. The popular kids think they have an advantage to bully us around just because of their looks. I think that they act that way to stay on top, so they can't be bullied or pushed around. That's how I feel about the bullying problems we have in school.

Bullies are age old, but maybe somehow scientists or someone can help with this problem. A quote on a church billboard says, "Kind words is the kind of way to go." Maybe if people spread this around school instead of rumors and bad names, then maybe it would help with our bully problem. So I think kind words is the way to go!!

By Lorna Abner, 12
Valley View Middle School
Germantown, OH

The Victim

Shiny instruments lay strewn about the carpeted floor in the GHS band room. Noise engulfed the room, filled with the taunting shouts of the band members. In the middle of the room stood a shrimpy looking freshman with thick glasses complete with heavy rims. In a minute he was off again, chasing the bully who now held his tattered band music. The students chanted awful things, urging him to go run and get it. Seeing as he was not exactly the quickest person, everyone already knew that he had no hope. But never the less, he kept running.

Discreetly while the poor boy was on the run, a chair was placed in the middle of his path. The chair just sat there asking to be tripped over. At a high rate of speed, the boy charged over the chair, and at the last moment tripped over the leg, and flew off onto the floor. For a moment, he just lay there sprawled in a heap, helpless, and unable to defend him. All around him, the laughter echoed. The ridicule began to subside, when a voice spoke out.

"Guys, why did you do that, just leave him alone," said the assertive voice. "What, do you like love him or something?" Jimmy chanted.

"Ooooooh, you love Curtis." The class moaned.

"No, guys, it's just not right, and if y'all do not know that, then ... "

She was interrupted mid sentence by the band teacher who was urging students back to their seats. As students were filing back to their seats, one lone student separated themselves from the group, and helped him up. Even though I witnessed a person being severely bullied, I made no attempt to dissuade them, and to this day, I feel guilty. Thank goodness for the other students who did.

This relates to the Kitty Genovese theory because, since there was a group of students surrounding him, they all thought "Oh, someone else will stop it." But, now we know that usually, people won't, and the best thing to do is stand up for the person. Afterwards you'll feel great, and know you did the right thing.

By Emily Bees, 15
Glastonbury High School
Glastonbury, CT

How I Can Prevent Bullying

Bullying is a child's worst nightmare, a child's worst fear. Bullying is common in schools now-a-days, and has always been present. No matter what you wear or where you come from, certain people will naturally be a target for bullies.

WindyRidge has its popular and non-popular groups. It's bullies and it's victims. Though there is The Bully Prevention Program, it still doesn't and never will stop bullying. Many serious cases this year have occurred, and none have seen the truth. WindyRidge is a small school, like a small town, where everyone knows everything about you, even though most of it is not true. When rumors go around, just like at every other school, it usually starts with collusion. Collusion is when someone in the group starts bullying a victim and the bully wants one of their buddies to join in.

This is what happens at WindyRidge. The popular or well liked kids pick on or bully the kids that are known to be different. Then they start by simply looking at them funny or looking at them and whispering hateful and cruel things. Usually one of the kids in the group were one of victims at one point and understand what they're going through, and usually one of the victims used to be their friend. For the sake of being popular or well liked, they go along with their group in the bullying not caring or recognizing how much they have hurt the victim(s).

In writing this I feel one way that I can help our school to be a collusion-free school is, not going along with this behavior and teaching every student to be aware of the consequences of bullying.

Being bullied is very tragic especially when it repeatedly happens even after being addressed. This may lead up to self-mutilation, suicide and or school shootings. Many students after being bullied so many times end up being the bad students, the misunderstood ones, the crazy ones.

My theory on all school shootings and incidents is that if you just listen to what the victims are screaming out, then you'll understand what is going on inside their heads and can prevent what is about to happen. Not listening to what the victims are saying or just strictly judging them or stereotyping them is just as bad as bullying them. In many cases like the famous Columbine incident, the students were bullied, stereotyped and tormented at school. This was what many specialists have said led up to the Columbine shooting. I believe there was a way this tragedy could have been prevented by more effective communication between the perpetrators and their parents and teachers. By saying this I will help and befriend someone in need because of bullying and will listen to what they have to say.

You can never stop bullying, even if you're an adult and or a child or even the President of the United States. It will always surround you, everywhere you go and every place you see. Bullying is something to make you feel powerful and stronger than the person you are bullying, and for the slight second you bully you feel like all your troubles are gone and the victim has taken them in. It is an addiction and a cruel one at that. You will see a form of bullying on TV and even cartoons and commercials. The advertisers want you to think, for example, if you don't wear Hollister or Nike then you're not in or cool so then you are basically bullied to dress like that and not be yourself so you can be in and not bullied when really you are.

I am writing this with the intention to help our school be bully-free and I for one, will never bully anyone.

Bullying will always happen and can never be stopped but it can prevented. By vowing to yourself, to never be a bully, and by vowing to yourself to never be a victim, and by always standing up for yourself, in a mature way, you can help stop bullying.

By Morgan Elisabeth Ayers, 14
WindyRidge Kindergarten through
8th, Orlando, FL

Big Nose Blues

Bullying is never a fun experience, I should know. My seventh grade year was an incredibly difficult and hurtful year at Dawson County Middle School. It was my second year at DCMS and I thought things were going pretty well. I had friends. Teachers were welcoming. I figured Dawson was a nice, accepting small county, and I was right. However, I can't quite say all the students were as welcoming as others.

I will never forget how my trip down Bully Lane began. My friends and I were sitting eating lunch one day and they were asking me how I liked Dawson so far. I told them it was nice and quiet, just the way I like it. They were asking me typical questions any teenage girl would ask, "Have you seen any boys you like, do you think so and so is cute, etc." They pointed out one boy and asked me if I thought he was cute. I told them, assuming they wouldn't tell anyone, that I didn't think so and I said something really mean about what he looked like. This is where my nightmare began.

Well, of course that wasn't the right thing to do, because one of them ended up telling him what I said. He got mad, and spread a real nasty rumor about me calling me ugly and saying I have a big nose. At first he only told his group of friends. Of course people around them heard and they figured, "hey they are teasing that girl maybe I should too!" Eventually, that incredibly hurtful rumor got around the entire seventh grade! My friends were even laughing at me behind my back! People started coming up with mean names such as elephant trunk, anchor nose, big one, and Mt. Everest. Sometimes people would even walk by me and start making elephant noises.

This is very hard to share with people. I realize the mental scars I still have. Today, I am an eighth-grade student on the basketball team, captain of the softball team, I participate in FCA, drama, and a straight A student. Things are going very well for me now. I have many more friends than I did last year and I am very happy. Fortunately, the teasing, and the names have all stopped except for the very rare, couple of statements that a few mean and immature people will say from time to time.

At first it was easier said than done, but I learned if you have enough going for you like friends, good grades, and sports then you will be set. So my advice to those being bullied is who cares what others think, just be yourself and stick with your pals and nothing that anybody else says about you will seem to matter any more.

By Amanda Daly, 13
Dawson County Middle School
Dawsonville, GA

Examples

It was a Saturday afternoon and my family had decided to go to the neighborhood park. We had been there for maybe an hour and a half, when some kids showed up. There were two older boys and two young girls. Twenty minutes from this time one of the little girls started screaming.

In alarm we looked over and saw that she was being abused. The older boys were throwing rocks (sand) in the little girls face. As wrong as it seemed we couldn't do anything but ask for them to please stop. So we went over to confront them! My mother went and asked politely if they would stop. The boys looked up at her and said "No she's our family, just leave us alone!" They continued to throw rocks at the little girl. Again my mother asked "Please, leave her alone."

After the second time of asking, the boys ran home and to their mother. The boys mother came and asked what the problem was. My mother then said "M'am, your boys were throwing rocks at this young lady!"

As soon as my mother was done speaking the boys mother said "We will do what we will with our family." Then she threw rocks in the little girls face and told my mother that if she didn't like it that she needed to do something about it! Of course my mother caring so much she had to call the police in safety of the child. After the women was done cursing at everyone she left and took the kids with her. I think the point of this story is that bullying isn't right whether its family or someone you just met!

My theory is that bullying is passed from generations, and I'm not talking about genetics. If you were a child who was raised around that do you think that you would grow up to do the same thing? I do!

Bullying is anger whether it is at yourself, your parents, or the kid that sits next to you in biology! If you were taught to bully others that is what you think is right. If your parents bully others and you see this it is a good example of what you might turn out as! But not necessarily.

I think there needs to be a respect program which teaches kids how to treat fellow students and/or parents.

In conclusion: be positive, respect others' feelings and listen to your surroundings because you can make a change, you can do anything.

By Alyssa Tia Sherer, 15
Highland High School
Pocatello, ID

Chapter: 10
The Bully

How can you help your school stop the bullying epidemic? To get started see the personal and School Action Plans here: http://www.mindoh.com/CB_registration.aspx

PS: Email us at info@mindohfoundation.org and tell us how your school got behind your Action Plan. We'll put it in a special section on our web site. Your story might even be in our next book! So start a campaign for anti-bullying on your campus now!

The Truth That Lies Beneath

It is not easy to be completely honest about yourself when writing things that you know will be viewed by others, but I will do my best to portray myself in the most truthful manner. It is quite ironic how seemingly innocent people can be the most vicious bullies when provoked, or even when not provoked. I was one of those "innocent" people, along with the other eighth graders of school bus Number Four. All eight of us had a lot in common – we attended the same elementary school and we also all lived in the same type of neighborhoods. We came from normal families that never really struggled with anything; we all were exceptional students. Despite our vast common ground, every single one of us managed to make enemies within the group. The alliances always fluctuated.

One instance that I recall with immense [un]ease is when the school year of 2004 had just rolled around. As usual the morning and afternoon bus rides always consisted of nasty comments that stretched the limits of teasing and cruelty, but this time, that limit had been surpassed with no remorseful thoughts. On the afternoon route, Joel and Kathleen were the first to be dropped off. At this time, the current standing for alliances was brutal: The majority of the group was against Joel. To be forthright and blatantly honest, Joel was not the skinniest boy, or good looking, for that matter. In seventh grade, Lori and I had done this after school cross country program, where we would try our best to get in shape. Joel had joined this group, and did his best to keep pace, to shed his unneeded extra weight. He always managed to hold the group back, and from then on, in both my eyes and Lori's, Joel was just the lazy, fat kid.

Since Joel was not exactly the most popular boy on our bus, even some of the seventh graders picked on him. As he was exiting the bus, the words "Joellie Ollie!" was sung out loud by one of the seventh graders, making a reference to the chubby Disney character from the show "Rollie Pollie Ollie". From that point on, whenever Joel was making entering or leaving our bus, the theme song of that show would be sung out by all of the bus' occupants, with of course, a few changes with the song. "Joellie Ollie Pollie! He's big and round and fat ... " He took the jabs with good humor, or he seemed to. The fact that he had made an effort in seventh grade to lose weight, showed that he was insecure with his size. But he hid his emotions and laughed, as almost all of us did whenever we were being targeted. Then again, I wasn't really picked on last year, for I was one of the "bigger" bullies. I wasn't the ringleader although I was high up.

The next day on the afternoon route, Tom came over to my seat and was holding his backpack in his arms, making kissing sounds ... and the sexual innuendos progressed, or, digressed – however you would want to look at it. It was only later that I found out that Lori had told him to do that to humiliate me. I didn't know what was going on, but I realized that my group had betrayed me that day. It stung me to realize that I truly had no alliances within that group, and I knew that I would have just as easily done the same to Lori, or anybody else, and plant the group on him or her without any backwards thoughts.

Even though I was hurt by this experience, and I knew that it was bad and horrible to do such a thing, I continued the torment, always telling myself everything was in good nature. We all convinced ourselves that we were just funny people with a sick sense of humor. The thing that shocks me and disgusts me, as I look back at my past, is that last year, our middle school was making an enormous emphasis on bullying. "Bullying is bad, for the insecure people." What shocks me even more is that we never got caught. To prevent further bullying instances from happening once more, I believe that the society should place a bigger emphasis on bullies and the hurt that they precipitate, and how people try to shrug off that pain and hide it with their own nasty remarks... almost like Newton's law of, "For every action, there is an equal and opposite reaction."

By Katelin Chow, 14
Glastonbury High school
Glastonbury, CT

Bullying - Can the Problem Be Solved?

I felt frustrated, helpless and embarrassed. I felt like a quitter. And it had happened over a year ago. Bullying certainly has the capacity to cause emotional harm. But as I had yet to fully realize, such damage can only last with the silent consent of the bullied. It is up to him to deny the self-blame which comes from a bullying situation, and to decide not to live the rest of his life under the shadow of that incident.

I was a twelve-year-old Boy Scout, just beginning to work toward the rank of Eagle Scout. But the organization of my troop made it all but impossible to advance in rank. My patrol leaders, older scouts responsible for helping the younger scouts complete requirements for advancing in rank, only worsened the situation. When you sought their help in completing a requirement you were either repulsed with shouting and ridicule or, if they were compelled to work with you, treated like an inferior being when you couldn't tie a knot correctly on the first try. In short, they bullied anyone who interrupted their hangout time, and yet you could never accomplish anything.

After a year, I decided to quit. Yet, though I hardly even

knew it, I continued to let the bullying get to me. I still felt embarrassed. I felt frustrated that I had not been able to achieve Eagle Scout.

I was a twelve years old, while the bullies were fifteen or sixteen years olds. Their positions as patrol leaders made their help necessary for advancing in rank. Quitting was my only good option. My fault was that I allowed the embarrassment and frustration to last. Once I got away from the bullies, it became my responsibility to eradicate the emotions caused by bullying.

One has only to reason, either by oneself or with someone else. Am I to blame for any part of what happened? Do I really have anything to be embarrassed about? If not, one must only remember this; if so, the situation can be considered a lesson for future reference. In either case, a past bullying situation need not have a negative effect on the rest of a person's life.

Bullying can cause two types of harm: physical and emotional. It seems ironic that in most cases the longer lasting and more damaging of the two is emotional, the type which is in the victim's control. Bullying itself is not likely to disappear from the face of the Earth any time soon. But by dealing right away with the emotional hurt that follows a bullying situation, it is possible to render bullying no more than an annoyance.

By Christopher Johnson, 14
Home schooled
Chester, NJ

Bullying Surrounds Me Every Day

Bullying is when someone intimidates another person for no good reason. I am surrounded by bullying every day. Each day when I come to school I always witness another person getting bullied. I do feel bad for not doing anything about it, but I always choose to just stay out of it. I'm not really sure if that makes me a bully also or no, but I try my hardest to not be a bully. I try to not be a bully because I know that some people get really offended by it and can get to the point where they just can't take it anymore and go crazy. I know from a personal experience how offended some people get by simply being teased by their appearance, personality, or even just by the way they talk.

A few years ago, when I was in 5th grade there was this girl who didn't have too great of a life. Her family didn't have much money so she didn't always have the best clothes and things like that. Due to her family being so hateful, this girl also had a lot of hate inside of her. She would release all of this hate on the people who made fun of her. The main reasons why people made fun of her was because of the way she looked and talked. She was from Texas so she had a light accent, and certain words made it stand out more. She always got made fun of for that reason. Another main reason was because she supposedly had big "rabbit teeth". When the kids would make fun of her for any of those reasons she would get so mad and sometimes to the point of tears. After a while, she began cutting herself because she just wasn't satisfied with anything going on in her life, and the teasing surely wasn't helping. People still never realized how much their teasing was hurting her, so they continued. Finally, the girl and her family moved away.

Now looking back at all of this, I just don't know how I was ever a part of any of this. Even though I hardly ever made a comment about her, but just the fact that I laughed along makes me feel ashamed of myself. All I can say now is that I hope that girl's life turned out okay, and that I always try my hardest to not have any part in bullying, even if it's just laughing along. In conclusion, all bullying does is harm people, and all together it's no good and people shouldn't bully at all.

By Jennifer Dragobratovich, 14
Buras Middle School
Buras, LA

Bully or Buddy

Bully or buddy. What do you want? I would definitely want buddy. It is still my opinion but I will just say that you need to be a buddy, not bully. I can tell some facts about why the buddies are better than bullies. I also can tell you that bullies are the worst things between friends. Sometimes bullies can be worse than the bad drugs.

Your choice between bully and buddy can make you happy or not. Bullying will always hurt your friend's feeling or yourself but the friends will always make you happy. If you are a bully your friends might leave you. You can be alone. People who care for you might be your family. You can think that people who are bullying someone with you are your friends but they can leave you anytime they want. Like if you guys are in trouble, they might blame it on you. If you are a buddy, you will be happy. You will find a true friend who always cares for you and also some who you care for.

Sometimes, bullies can be scary. It can kill people. If you bully a person with his or her characteristics, this person can think that he is nothing to anyone. This person might feel alone and if this situation continues, he may suicide.

Bullies also make a person crazy. When a person is bullied, that person can be come a murderer. These are how the bullies can be scary.

If you are being a bully, it means that you are losing. If you are being a bully, you will lose your friends first. They will leave you because of your behavior. If you lose your friends, you will lose your happiness and love. If you lose your happiness and love, you may lose your family. You may leave your family because you lost your love. If you lose your family, you will lose everything.

These are the reasons that it is not good to be a bully. I don't think you want to be a bully now. If you are a bully already, there is only one solution for it. Be a buddy not a bully. If you become a buddy you can be happy and earn something, not lose it. Be a buddy. Go up to a person or people that you bullied and apologize to them. Be a buddy with them. I think that is the only one solution for it.

By Youngmin Park, 14
Franklin Middle School
Nutley, NJ

The Girl I Used To Be

My family and I were all sitting around the TV watching home videos. My sister and I were very young throughout the videos. I was about four. As I watched how I acted when I was a little girl, I felt ashamed. What I was watching was one of the bossiest little brats. I controlled everyone that I was playing with and everything had to go my way. My parents and I were all laughing at how stubborn I was when I was a little girl. It's funny to watch it now, but at the time, I don't know how my parents or friends could deal with me. I know that that was just the way I was and didn't really mean to offend anyone, but if I were the one being bullied I'd be upset. My mother told me that one time my kindergarten teacher had called home to my parents telling them of how I bossed some of the kids around. To hear that made me laugh, but I was also surprised that my teacher actually had to call my house and tell my parents of my behavior. I had never known that she had done that until about a year ago. My mom said that it wasn't a big deal, I was just a pain.

Looking back at when I was about four or five years old, I can remember some of the things that I did. One day, my

friend Emily was over at my house to play for the afternoon. We were best friends in kindergarten. She was also
very bossy, just like me. The day she came over, we were
playing outside. My mom had filled up our little kiddy pool
for us to swim in. I had a neighbor who lived down the
street from me. We played together at school and sometimes out of school, but some things that she did really
annoyed me. I don't even remember what she did that bothered me so much, but it probably was nothing even important. I can remember many times when I wasn't always the
nicest person to her.

That day that Emily was over, Sophie came over to play
with us. The whole time Emily and I avoided her as if she
wasn't even there. I can't even imagine how awkward she
must have felt being at someone else's house and being
ignored. I'm surprised that she didn't just walk back home.
I knew that she had been crying. Emily and I just laughed.
Now that I think back to that day, I can't even explain my
actions. I don't understand how I could have been that
mean to someone so innocent.

Now when I talk to some of the friends that I was friends
with back then, they say how I was mean to them, but now
we just laugh about it. No one can ever believe me when I
say that at one time I was a little bully. I would never do
anything like I did when I was little to other people now.
When I'm babysitting or with my cousins and there are
other little kids that they're playing with, who are bossing
them around, I always stick up for the ones being bullied.
When I watch those home videos with my family, I feel like
slapping the girl on the TV. I was so annoying and controlling; I don't know how other kids could have dealt with me.
When I think of it now, I just think that it was a stage that
I was going through and luckily grew out if it by first grade.

I could never even imagine bullying anyone now. As I grew older, I became shyer but still outgoing. I wasn't as wild and crazy as I was in kindergarten. I was nice and played well with other kids, instead of controlling them.

by Mary Ann Presutti, 14
Glastonbury High School
Glastonbury, CT

Looking Up To A Bully

"Sticks and stones will break my bones, but words will never hurt me." Everyone has heard someone say this or said it themselves, but it is grossly incorrect. Both harsh words and kind words have a more lasting affect than physical pain. How we are viewed; how we are spoken of by others helps shape our own perceptions of ourselves. When the people we look up to, hurt us, however, it is much worse than anything our friends or strangers could do. And I have been on both ends of bullying.

Though there may be harsher forms of bullying, when someone you look up to puts you down, it is one of the worst possible feelings. I have experienced this from an upper classmen I know. We were often weight lifting at the same time, and though I don't know why, he would tease me. Things like "What are you doing here?" or singling me out during pickup games. And though these things may seem trivial, it hurts when someone you once looked up to is now aiming at you above any other target, with both games and words.

Nevertheless, I have done similar things to kids younger than me and I have witnessed it done to others. Teasing them for the kind of clothes they wear or their weight or some insignificant habit hurts; they, however, like me, try to hide it. This is something I can try to stop, beginning with what I say to the younger kids looking to me for guidance. I know from personal experience how much a kind word can mean; when someone, especially someone you admire, appreciates you as well.

Unfortunately, bullying will never end, but when we are prepared and understand what it truly is and how it feels, we can be armed to defend and fight against it. The message against bullying has come to the forefront in schools; there are lectures and groups in every school that encourage us to support each other, stop bullying, and to do the "right" thing. Yet the successful businessmen, politicians, and athletes we see outside of school seem to have no sense of this morality. All things considered, why would students strive against the rest of the world to be morally right without a higher purpose? In a time when traditional morality is often labeled bigotry and intolerance, what moral code is there?

By Kristofer J. Thompson, 16
Thompson Homeschool
Succasunna, NJ

5th Grade Bully

One day, my friend, Marissa, said, "Someone's bullying me." "What?" "Someone said they were going to beat me up tomorrow after school," she said. "You're only a 2nd grader and somebody wants to beat you up? Want did you ever do to them?" I said. Then the bell rang, "DING, DING, DING!" "Well," I said, "We might want to go tell the teacher and then the principal." I said. Marissa agreed.

As soon as we got into Mrs. Reddick's class, Marissa and I told her about this kid and how they were going to beat her up after school. Mrs. Reddick said, "I'm going to tell the principal, Mrs. Meashia, about this kid that wants to beat you up." "See Marissa, I told you everything will be fine," I said. She was so worried the whole day, but I was with her the whole time. Marissa felt better to know that I would be there with her to protect her.

When the bell rang to go, my mom came to pick me up from school. I told her what was going to happen and we went straight to the principal's office to report about the kid that was going to beat Marissa up tomorrow after school. The principal said, "We will have ADs on the playground, on the field, in front of the school, and all around campus." "Thank you," Marissa said. Then, Marissa's mom came and took her home.

The next day, Marissa was still a little worried, but knew she was safe. The teacher, Mrs. Reddick, said she had filed a report about the kid. The day went by so fast then, the bell rang to go home, "DING, DING, DING!" Marissa was real nervous now, by the look on her face. I walked her out of the room and all of a sudden, a big, mean, 5th grader came up behind us and swung at us. "Run, run, run," I said.

We were running so fast that we were like a 100-mile car! The weird thing was that there were no teachers around. Marissa and I ran up to the front of the school where the ADs were supposed to be. Nobody was there! "Ahhhhhhhhh!" Marissa and I screamed. The 5th grader was right behind us. Just then there was a miracle, an AD was 50 feet away from us. We started screaming so the AD could hear us. The AD saw the kid running after us and she asked us if we were OK. Then after we said, "Yes," she took the kid up to the principal's office and he got suspended for going to beat up Marissa. She said, "Thank you Megan for all your help, you are such a great friend." "I'm so glad he didn't hurt you." Then, our moms took us home and nobody has hurt Marissa again.

What I will do to stop bullying is not get involved in bullying and help my friends not get involved either. I'm going to try to get on a leadership and make a program for kids that bully other people and make them not want to bully anymore. Hopefully, this will happen and the schools will be a better place to learn and make new friends.

By Megan Faherty, 11
Thompson Middle School
Murrieta, CA

Bullying is a Very Big Deal in Schools

Bullying is a very big deal in schools today. It causes kids to undergo pain, sadness and loss of self-esteem. Many people say it is for attention, but I think it is because of the lack of friends in a person's life. I know this because I once was a bully. When I actually got a friend I had no reason to be a bully anymore. So, as you can see that is the main reason why I think people become bullies is to try and get some friends.

A bully harms himself and the victim. The victim gets physically harmed and the bully gets emotionally harmed. The bully gets depressed and loses self-esteem, and so does the victim. They are both hurt and lose the respect for others that they use to have.

Bullying can lead to bad choices in the future. Like joining gangs or getting into gun wars. So when one of your friends becomes a bully you need to help them out and try to get them on the right path again. Bullying can also lead to drugs, alcohol, and smoking. So you need to help your friends as soon as you can.

Bullying can also come from their family. They may come from a household where their family is always fighting

They can also come from lack of friends, to get attention, and to try and get popular. If you know someone who is a bully, try to help them. Ask them why they act the way they do and try to help them get better and be able to not bully.

As you can see there are many ways that people become bullies. Many have tried, but no one has really figured out the exact reason why people become bullies.

By Anthony James Smith, 13
Forney Middle School
Forney, TX

Little Bullies

Have you ever been bullied by someone? Almost everyone in the world has been teased or bullied in their life. I remember a time in the first grade when I was teased because of my last name. My last name is Little, and those that bullied me were relentless. As a young child, I wished so much that I could change my last name to Smith or Johnson just so the bullies would leave me alone. Most people have felt something similar to those things that I was feeling at the time. Bullies leave marks of shame, embarrassment, and low self esteem on their victims.

As I was ridiculed for my last name, I became very ashamed of it. I hated telling people my full name because I felt that if they knew my last name, they would judge me and tease me. I began to have feelings of jealousy toward my friends who had last names like Anderson or Hall. I would have done anything to switch names with them.

In addition to feeling ashamed, I sometimes harbored feelings of embarrassment. When I was asked what my full name was, I would proudly proclaim my first name and shyly mutter my last. I was very embarrassed to let others know my full name. Even though they probably wouldn't have said anything, I still felt as though they might exclude me in some way or another solely for the reason that my last name was Little. I began asking people to just call me by my first name, Janet.

Soon the shame and embarrassment that I felt led to me becoming very critical of myself. I began to tear myself down in every aspect. It was no longer just my last name that bothered me. I hated the way I talked and the way I walked. Although the bullies might not have thought much about it when they were teasing me, their words were like daggers to my self esteem.

Bullies leave marks of shame, embarrassment, and low self esteem on their victims. Most bullies aren't fully aware of the pain caused from their words and actions. In some situations, the effects are life altering. Fortunately, I've come to terms with the pain my bullies caused me, and I'm now able to laugh with those that laugh at my last name.

by Janet Little, 16
Highland High School
Pocatello, ID

The Look

Walking around the halls in my school is almost like taking a "bully tour". Everywhere you look, whether it be a bathroom or a deserted stairwell, bullies are taking advantage of younger kids and those who don't fit in. Seeing as no one does much about it, the bullying is ceaseless. However, one instance of bullying that I witnessed struck me as so cruel that it has stayed with me until this day.

For the most part, bullies tend to stay away from my friends and I, allowing us freedom of movement throughout the school halls. For one kid, however, this was not the case. This student walked through the halls with a rolling backpack, and this didn't help the thick glasses that he wore, nor the accent that affected his speech.

"Hey – you little s*** over there! Give me your wallet!"

Naturally, the kid handed over his wallet, hoping it would buy him passage to his next class, where he could hide behind the safety of the teacher's trouble-searching eyes. But, the wallet was not enough to get him to the next class. "What the hell? There's only three bucks in here? Are you trying to buy your own mom for a night?"

While it wasn't quite public knowledge, one of our teachers had told us in class that the kid's mom had died two weeks earlier. Realizing that this could be a bad situation, I decided to step in.

"Dude, back off. Get your own money."

Alone, I probably wouldn't have been able to do such a thing, but, backed by my friends, I felt a little more brave. Seeing that there were six of us, and only one of him, the bully shot us a glare and backed away. The kid took the opportunity to scamper off to the next class, but not before he gave me a look I will never forget.

In his eyes I saw such gratitude that it overcame the fear still etched on his face. Nobody has ever looked at me in such a way, and I felt like I had just saved the world. I will never forget that look and now I know what I have to do when I witness bullying because it really means something.

By Michael Willen, 15
Glastonbury High School
Glastonbury, CT

Permissions

"Cursive Names" Reprinted by permission of Lorna Abner © 2005 Lorna Abner

"Bullying is An Issue" Reprinted by permission of Courtney Andries © 2005 Courtney Andries

"How I Can Prevent Bullying" Reprinted by permission of Morgan Elisabeth Ayers © 2005 Morgan Elisabeth Ayers

"The Victim" Reprinted by permission of Emily Bees © 2005 Emily Bees

"Hurting Someone's Feelings is Worse Than What You Think" Reprinted by permission of Jeremy B. Buhain © 2005 Jeremy B. Buhain

"The Act of Kindness" Reprinted by permission of Tyson Bybee © 2005 Tyson Bybee

"What Every Big Sister Wants" Reprinted by permission of Amanda Carey © 2005 Amanda Carey

"Bullying" Reprinted by permission of Jeffrey Carter © 2005 Jeffrey Carter

"Infect the World with Peace" Reprinted by permission of Zi Wen Chen © 2005 Zi Wen Chen

"The Truth That Lies Beneath" Reprinted by permission of Katelin Chow © 2005 Katelin Chow

"The Three Things I Will Do" Reprinted by permission of Carmen Adriana Clemente © 2005 Carmen Adriana Clemente

"Bullies - A Problem Waiting to Be Solved" Reprinted by permission of Kathryn A. Costidis © 2005 Kathryn A. Costidis

"Big Nose Blues" Reprinted by permission of Amanda Daly © 2005 Amanda Daly

"Skin Deep" Reprinted by permission of Tram Dao © 2005 Tram Dao

2005 Contest Participants

Students and schools across the country participated in the 2005 Character's Cool Contest. The winning school with the most survey entries was **D.A. Smith Middle School** in Ozark, Alabama (a former runner up!) and the runner up for 2005 was **East Hanover Middle School** in East Hanover, New Jersey. The following schools participated in the Survey portion. Additional schools and states participated in the Essay Contest. Congratulations!

ALABAMA

D.A. Smith MS *

ALASKA

T.J Erdl Madrt

ARIZONA

Barcelona Middle School
Glassford Hill Middle School

ARKANSAS

Murfreesboro High School
Union High School

Washington Middle School

CALIFORNIA

Christ the King
Desert Mirage High School
Ethel Dwyer Middle School
Golden Valley Charter School
Herbert Hoover Middle School
Hillside Middle School
Marina Middle School
McKinleyville Middle School
Palos Verdes Peninsula HS
Peterson Alt Center for Education
Presidio Middle School
Righetti High School
Royal High School

Sequoia Middle School
Suzanne Middle School
Theodore Roosevelt
Thompson Middle School
Twenty-nine Palms Junior High
Warm Springs Middle School

CONNECTICUT

Bethel Middle School
Glastonbury High School
Jared Eliot

DELAWARE

Gunning Bedford MS
Laurel Senior High School
Sussex Central High School

FLORIDA

Christa McAuliffe MS
Crestwood Middle School
H.L. Watkins Middle School
Lecanto High School
North Fort Myers High School
Pierce Middle School
Robert Hungerford Prep High
Saint Edwards School
Sebastian River Middle School
Veterans Park Acad for the Arts
Villa Madonna Catholic School
West Port High School
Windy Ridge Elementary

GEORGIA

Appalachia High School
Burke County Middle School
Dawson County Middle School
Flat Rock Middle School

Grayson High School
Hart County Middle School
Miller Magnet Middle School
North Forsyth Middle School
Sandersville Elementary
T.J. Elder Middle School
Thompson Middle School
Ware County High
Winder Barrow Middle School

IDAHO

Franklin Middle School
Hawthorne Middle School
Highland High School
Home Schooled
Homedale High School
Indian Hills
Liberty Elementary School
New Horizon High School
Twin Falls High School

ILLINOIS

Casimir Pulaski Fine Arts Acad
Gibson City Melvin Sibley MS
Hinsdale Middle School

INDIANA

George Washington MS

KANSAS

Central Junior High School
Derby High School
Douglass High School
Free State High School
Hutchinson High School
Larned High School
Lawrence Free State HS

Pawnee Heights
Plainville High School
Robinson Middle School
Sisk Middle School
Smith Center Jr.-Sr. High School
Stafford High School
Wheatland High School

LOUISIANA

Buras Middle School
Haughton High School
Johnson River Middle School

MARYLAND

Broadneck High School
Colonel Richardson MS
Earle B. Wood Middle School
George Fox Middle School
Harford Technical High School
Lockerman Middle School
Montgomery College-
  Germantown Campus
Northeast High School
Rockville High School
The Caroline Career and
  Technology Center

MASSACHUSETTS

Boston Latin School

MICHIGAN

Bridgeport High School
Clinton High School
Boulan Park Middle School

MINNESOTA

St. Peter High School

MISSOURI

Washington Middle School
Harrisonville Middle School

MISSISSIPPI

Ocean Springs High School

MONTANA

Centerville
Fort Benton High School

NEBRASKA

McCook High School
Walnut Middle School

NEW JERSEY

Belleville Middle School
East Hanover MS **
Franklin Middle School
Home Educated
John Adams Middle School
John P Stevens High School
Lakeside Middle School
Linwood Middle School
Nutley High School
Perth Amboy High School
Plainfield High School
St. John The Apostle
Verona High School
Woodrow Wilson ES

NEW MEXICO

Cibola High School

NEW YORK

Adirondack Middle School
Adlai E. Stevenson HS
Amherst Middle School
Arcadia Middle School
Dake Jr. High
DeWitt Clinton High School
East Hampton High School
Hendrick Hudson High School
Herbert H. Lehman
Lackawanna Middle School
Otselic Valley Elementary
Sleepy Hollow Middle/HS
Smithtown Middle School
South Jefferson High School
The Boys' Club of New York
Abbe Clubhouse
Warm Springs Middle School

NORTH CAROLINA

Belmont, Middle School
East Chapel Hill High School
J.F. Webb High School
Western Alamance MS/HS

NORTH DAKOTA

Erik Ramstad Middle School
Longfellow
Magic City Campus
Memorial Middle School
Minot High School
Nathan Twining Middle School

OHIO

Canfield High School
Diley Middle School
Hope Academy East
John Marshall High School
Valley View Middle School

OKLAHOMA

Highland West Junior High
Jones Middle School
State Center Middle School

OREGON

Calapooia Middle School
Home School
Judson Middle School

PENNSYLVANIA

Abington Junior High School
Cedarbrook Middle School
Scott Middle School
Seneca Valley
Susquehanna High School

RHODE ISLAND

Charles E. Shea Sr High School
Mt. Pleasant High School

SOUTH CAROLINA

Greer High School
Pelion Middle School
Capitol High School

SOUTH DAKOTA

Wessington After School Program

TENNESSEE

Cleveland Middle School
Danielson Christian Academy

TEXAS

Allen High School
Alvarado High School
Atascocita Middle School
Aubrey High School
Barbara Jordan HS for Careers
Bellaire High School
Bowie High School
C.E. King High School
Corny Middle School
Corsicana High School
Forney Middle School
Fossil Ridge High School
Furr High School
Grapevine High School
Hall Middle School
Hargrave High School
Harlingen High School
Humble 9th Grade/HS
James Bowie High School
Jefferson Davis High School
Kingwood High School
L.E. Claybon Elementary
Lamar High School
Madisonville High School
Mance Park Middle School
Martin High School
McDonald Middle School
Oak Crest Intermediate
Ore City High School

Quitman High School
Riverwood Middle School
Seagoville Middle School
Shallowater High School
Shirley Hall Middle School
Sonora High School
Splendora High School
Utopia High School
Waltrip High School
Washington High School
Westbury Senior High School
Windsong Intermediate

VIRGINIA

Cave Spring High School
James River
L.F. Addington Middle School
St. Francis of Assisi
Vernon Johns Middle School

WASHINGTON

Forks High School
Kamiakin Junior High
Lakewood Middle School
Mihaly School
Rose Hill Junior High
White River High School

WEST VIRGINIA

Bridgeport Middle School

*   2005 Winner
** 2005 Runner-Up

Recommended Resources

DR. MARVIN BERKOWITZ

Marvin W. Berkowitz, the inaugural Sanford N. McDonnell Endowed Professor of Character Education at the University of Missouri-St. Louis, was previously the inaugural Ambassador Holland J. Coors Professor of Character Development at the United States Air Force Academy.

In his most recent book, *Parenting For Good*, he shows us that parenting is not for the faint-of-heart. In this book of essays, Dr. Berkowitz, one of character development's leading educators, offers his wit, wisdom, and experiences on the joys, surprises (and everything else in between) on raising children. This is a compilation of the best of Dr. Berkowitz's syndicated newspaper columns, offering insight, advice, and strategies for parents with kids of all ages. www.mindoh.com/Book_mberkowitz01.aspx

MARK VICTOR HANSEN

America's Ambassador of Possibility – In the area of human potential, no one is better known and more respected than Mark Victor Hansen. For more than 25 years, Mark has focused solely on helping people and organizations from all walks of life, reshape their personal vision of what's possible.

You may know Mark better as "that Chicken Soup for the Soul guy." The last handful of years has seen Mark, and his business partner Jack Canfield, create what TIME magazine calls "the publishing phenomenon of the decade." With more than 90 million Chicken Soup for the Soul books sold in North America alone and over 100 licensed products in the marketplace.

MINDOH!

MindOH! is a socially responsible company named for that moment when a child's belief in what is, and their belief in what can be, come together. The Company creates character-based, interactive computer modules that teach students problem-solving techniques and communication skills, reinforcing universally held virtues such as respect and responsibility. www.mindoh.com.

THE MINDOH! FOUNDATION

In 2001 MindOH! extended their commitment to character education by starting the MindOH! Foundation. Every year, the MindOH! Foundation sponsors the Character's Cool Contest which is a national, online contest for kids to reflect on what it means to have good character. Other initiatives have included free resources for parents and schools for Hurricane Katrina, the 2005 Tsunami affecting Asia and Africa, cyberbullying, the war in Iraq, the Columbia disaster and September 11th.

For your free cyberbullying and school violence tools visit www.mindohfoundation.org.

PROJECT WISDOM

Project Wisdom is one of the oldest and most respected character education programs in the nation. It's collection of daily words of wisdom is currently licensed to over 12,500 schools nationwide. The messages set a positive tone for the day for everyone on campus. This program imparts an understanding of core ethical values and fosters caring behavior. The centerpiece of the program is a collection of thought-provoking messages designed to be read over your PA or in-house television system. These messages inspire and teach. www.projectwisdom.com.

Building Moral Intelligence: www.moralintelligence.com

Character Education Partnership: www.character.org

ChildBuilders: www.childbuilders.org

Center for the 4th and 5th Rs: www.cortland.edu/character.index.asp

Cyberbullying and Anti-Violence Resources from MindOH!: www.mindoh.com/Cyberbullying.aspx

Mentoring.org: www.mentoring.org

Mothers Against Violence in America (MAVIA): www.mavia.org

Students Against Violence Everywhere (SAVE): www.saveusa.org

Tadpole Club: www.tadpoleclub.com

MindOH! and The Foundation

The MindOH! Foundation was founded in 2001 to provide young people, educators and parents with the necessary tools to help develop strong character traits and healthy self-concepts. The Foundation's main sponsor is MindOH!, an e-learning company that creates character-based, interactive tools to teach students problem-solving techniques and communication skills, reinforcing universally held virtues such as respect and responsibility.

Contributions to The MindOH! Foundation go to support the development and reinforcement of character education to improve student performance, decrease dropout rates, and make schools safer and more productive. The Foundation has seen success with past charitable campaigns such as its annual Character's Cool Contest which began in January 2002, and has since reached thousands of kids in the US and Canada. The 2005 Contest received mass media attention from news organizations such as CNN Headline News, People Magazine, USA Today, Time Magazine and the New York Post.

Additionally, The Foundation has provided resources to help students, teachers, and parents through difficult times such as September 11th, the Columbia space shuttle disaster, the war in Iraq and Hurricane Katrina. These tools serve as discussion guides to help children remember virtues such as respect, tolerance and compassion when facing a challenging time or tragedy.

To learn more about MindOH!'s products and services, please visit www.mindoh.com, and to learn more about the MindOH! Foundation, visit www.mindohfoundation.org.

The Character's Cool Contest

The Character's Cool Contest was dreamed up in a coffee shop in Seattle, Washington in 2001 as the first initiative under the newly formed MindOH! Foundation. It was a grass roots effort to bring together sponsors and schools and create a national program to teach our nation's youth about a fairly new concept in schools – character education.

2002 – Character Education

The first contest had a general theme about character education - what it was, how it applied to school, life and the world events. Most students ended up reflecting on world events. That year, 1,899 students completed the online survey, 303 students submitted essays and 130 schools participated in 35 states. Abington Middle School in Abington, PA won the grand prize and Cleveland Middle School in Cleveland, TN was the runner up.

2003 – Laws of Life

The second Contest saw participation increase dramatically with 6,503 survey participants, 591 essays from 277 schools in 37 states. We teamed up with the Laws of Life Essay Program with the John Templeton Foundation. The theme was: Love. Perseverance. Gratitude. Compassion.

Tomah Middle School in Tomah, WI won the grand prize and D.A. Smith Middle School in Ozark, AL was runner up.

2004 – Tolerance and Compassion

In 2004, students and adults around the country were thinking about world events, particularly the war in Iraq. That year's Contest theme was about tolerance and compassion. There were 5,939 survey participants, 1,321 essays with 335 schools in 45 states. A.I. Root Middle School in Medina, OH won the grand prize. Gibson City Melvin Sibley Middle School in Gibson City, IL was the runner up.

2005 – Bullying and Cyberbullying

Which leads us to the 2005 Contest theme that prompted the creation of our first book – bullying and cyberbullying. As mentioned earlier, the 2005 Contest had 5,502 survey entries, approximately 1,300 essay entries, with 250 schools in 45 states. This year, the grand prize school was D.A. Smith Middle School in Ozark, AL (formerly a runner up!) and the runner up was East Hanover Middle School in East Hanover, NJ.

Starting February 1, 2006

The 2006 Character's Cool Contest will be another chance for teens to share their stories and experiences, and to possibly be published in the 2006 issue of *Teens Tell It Like It Is* series. The Contest will be held throughout the month of February 2006, and will include new opportunities for schools and parents to get involved.

If you would like to receive an email reminder from The MindOH! Foundation on February 1st, visit the Web site at www.mindohfoundation.org/contest/ to sign up.

Jennifer O'Brien

2005 Contest Results

The 2005 Character's Cool Contest Survey had 5,502 participants and the Essay Contest had more than 1,300 students participate from 250 schools in 40 states. The Survey portion of the Contest asked students to think about bullying from three perspectives: the bully, the victim, and the bystander. Students selected reasons why some kids might bully, sympathized with the emotions a victim might feel and thought about the responsibilities one might have when watching a bullying situation.

Below you will find a sample of questions the students answered on the Survey portion. For a complete review of the entire Survey, go to: www.mindohfoundation.org/contest/2005_results.htm

---

What is your experience with bullying or teasing? Check as many as are true.

I have been the victim of bullying or teasing before.	57%
I have bullied or teased someone else before.	41%
I have watched as someone else was being bullied.	82%

In this modern day we have access to the Internet and other technology that make communication easier. It also provides more chances for kids to bully each other online and through cell phones. What are some examples that you have heard of kids cyberbullying each other?

Creating Web sites that make fun of others	50%
Taking cruel pictures with digital phones and sending them around	59%
Gossiping about others in online chat rooms	77%
Logging on using someone else's identity without their permission	54%
Sending anonymous messages or spreading rumors	78%

What are some things we can do to stop bullying? Select as many as you would like.

We could spend more time talking about how respectful behaviors help us, our families, our communities and the world.	54%
We could encourage kids to do the right thing by talking to an adult they trust when someone is being mistreated or bullied.	69%
We could anonymously report incidents of bullying to a trusted adult.	68%
We could spend more time putting ourselves in the place of those being bullied.	58%
We could learn ways to see things from another person's perspective.	68%
We could ask ourselves if we want to live in a world where hurtful behaviors are acceptable or where respectful behaviors are expected.	59%
We could always ask ourselves this question: "Is this the way I would want to be treated?"	75%